KITCHENAID STAND MIXER COOKBOOK

FOR BEGINNERS 2024

Delicious and Homemade Recipes for Bread, Cookies, Cakes, Ice Cream, Pasta, Doughs, Dips, Sauces, and Frostings

Marie Carr

1

Table of Contents

Introduction 8

World of Stand Mixers 10

Understanding Stand Mixer Settings and Speeds 10

Must-Have Accessories and Attachments 13

Tips for Using Your KitchenAid Stand Mixer 16

Care and Maintenance 16

Maximizing Efficiency and Performance 18

Breads 20

Classic White Bread 20

Whole Wheat Bread 23

Multigrain Bread 26

Sourdough Bread 29

Rye Bread 32

Ciabatta 35

Focaccia 38

Brioche 41

Bagels 44

English Muffins 47

Cookies 50

Chocolate Chip Cookies 50

Oatmeal Raisin Cookies 53

Peanut Butter Cookies 56

Snickerdoodles 58

Sugar Cookies 61

Double Chocolate Cookies 64

Gingerbread Cookies 67

Shortbread Cookies 70

Macarons 72

Biscotti 75

Cakes **78**

Classic Vanilla Cake 78

Chocolate Fudge Cake 80

Red Velvet Cake 82

Carrot Cake 84

Lemon Drizzle Cake 87

Angel Food Cake 90

Pound Cake 92

Bundt Cake 94

Cheesecake 96

Tiramisu Cake 98

Ice Cream **102**

Vanilla Bean Ice Cream 102

Chocolate Ice Cream 105

Strawberry Ice Cream 108

Mint Chocolate Chip Ice Cream 111

Cookies and Cream Ice Cream 114

Pistachio Ice Cream 117

Coffee Ice Cream 120

Mango Sorbet.. 123

Raspberry Gelato 125

Coconut Ice Cream 128

Pasta **132**

Classic Egg Pasta 132

Spinach Pasta 135

Whole Wheat Pasta 138

Gluten-Free Pasta.. 141

Ravioli with Ricotta Filling 144

Fettuccine Alfredo 147

Spaghetti Carbonara..................................... 149

Pappardelle with Bolognese......................... 151

Lasagna Sheets... 154

Gnocchi 156

Doughs... **158**

Pizza Dough 158

Calzone Dough... 161

Pretzel Dough... 164

Empanada Dough... 167

Tortilla Dough.. 170

Pita Bread Dough 172

Naan Bread Dough 175

Cinnamon Roll Dough 177

Donut Dough.. 180

Croissant Dough... 183

Dips and Sauces.. **186**

    Classic Hummus 186

    Spinach and Artichoke Dip.................................... 188

    Guacamole 190

    Salsa Verde 192

    Marinara Sauce 194

    Alfredo Sauce... 196

    Pesto Sauce 198

    BBQ Sauce.. 200

    Cheese Sauce 202

    Tzatziki 204

Frostings and Fillings **206**

    Buttercream Frosting 206

    Cream Cheese Frosting... 208

    Chocolate Ganache 210

    Lemon Curd 212

    Pastry Cream.. 214

Conclusion **216**

INTRODUCTION

Welcome to the "KitchenAid Stand Mixer Cookbook for Beginners 2024." If you're just starting out or looking to up your culinary game, this book is here to help you unlock the full potential of your KitchenAid stand mixer.

This versatile powerhouse can transform your kitchen experience, making baking and cooking not only easier but also more enjoyable.

Imagine effortlessly kneading dough for fresh, homemade bread, whipping up light and fluffy meringues, or even grinding meat for your own gourmet burgers. This book is designed to turn those possibilities into reality. I'll provide you with the tips, techniques, and recipes you need to become a master of your mixer.

From the moment you unbox your stand mixer, it can seem a bit overwhelming with all its settings and attachments. This book breaks everything down in a straightforward, easy-to-understand way.

You'll learn about the various speed settings and how each one can be used to achieve perfect results every time. I'll guide you through essential maintenance tips to keep your mixer in top condition, ensuring it lasts for years to come.

One of the best features of the KitchenAid stand mixer is its range of attachments. We'll explore the most useful ones, showing you how they can expand the versatility of your mixer.

Whether you're making pasta from scratch, grinding your own meat, or creating perfectly spiralized vegetables, these attachments will take your culinary skills to the next level. Of course, no cookbook would be complete without recipes, and this one is packed with delicious options. From basic bread recipes to more complex dishes, each recipe is designed to showcase what your mixer can do. You'll find clear, step-by-step instructions that make it easy to follow along and achieve great results.

As a passionate home cook and baking enthusiast, I've spent countless hours experimenting with my KitchenAid stand mixer. This book is a culmination of my experiences, trials, and triumphs in the kitchen. My goal is to share this knowledge with you, helping you create delicious, professional-quality dishes with ease.

This book is more than just a collection of recipes; it's a comprehensive guide to making the most of your KitchenAid stand mixer. Whether you're looking to perfect your baking skills or try out new cooking techniques, you'll find a variety of what you are looking for right here.

So, grab your apron, plug in your mixer, and let's embark on this exciting culinary journey together. Welcome to a world of endless possibilities and delicious results. Happy mixing.

WORLD OF STAND MIXERS

Understanding Stand Mixer Settings and Speeds

To truly unlock KitchenAid stand mixer potential, you need to understand its settings and speeds. Let's dive in and get to know it better.

The Basics of Stand Mixer Settings

Your stand mixer comes with various speed settings, each designed for specific tasks. These settings help you achieve the perfect consistency and texture for your recipes. Here's a quick overview:

- **Stir Speed (Speed 1):** This is the slowest setting, perfect for gentle mixing. Use it for stirring dry ingredients together, combining ingredients slowly, or when starting the mixer with a lot of flour to avoid a mess. It's also great for slow kneading.

- **Slow Mixing (Speed 2):** This speed is ideal for slow mixing and kneading doughs. It's great for cookie dough, heavier batters, and mashing potatoes. It provides enough power to mix ingredients thoroughly without overworking them.

- **Medium Low (Speed 4):** This setting is perfect for mixing cake batters, cookie dough, and brownie batter.

It ensures ingredients are well combined without incorporating too much air, which can affect the texture of baked goods.

- **Medium (Speed 6):** Use this speed for creaming butter and sugar together until light and fluffy. It's also great for mixing frostings and beating eggs.
- **Medium High (Speed 8):** This speed is designed for whipping cream, beating egg whites, and making meringues. It incorporates a lot of air, giving you light and airy mixtures.
- **High (Speed 10):** The highest speed is rarely needed but is perfect for those times when you need to whip something very quickly and incorporate maximum air. Use it cautiously to avoid overmixing.

Choosing the Right Speed for the Task

Understanding which speed to use can make a big difference in your results.

- **Stirring:** Use Speed 1 for gentle mixing. It's perfect for stirring in ingredients that could easily get overmixed or for starting a mix to prevent flour from flying everywhere.
- **Mixing:** Speed 2 is ideal for mixing and kneading doughs. It provides enough power to mix heavy ingredients without overworking the dough, making it perfect for bread and pizza doughs.
- **Creaming:** Speed 4 is your go-to for creaming butter and sugar. This speed creates a light and fluffy mixture, essential for many baked goods.

- **Beating:** Speed 6 is great for beating and mixing. Use it for cake batters and cookie doughs where you need a bit more power to combine ingredients thoroughly.
- **Whipping:** Speed 8 is designed for whipping. It's perfect for making whipped cream and meringues, where you need to incorporate a lot of air quickly.
- **High-Speed Whipping:** Speed 10 is the fastest setting, ideal for whipping small quantities of cream or egg whites very quickly.

Tips for Effective Mixing

1. **Start Slow:** Always start at a lower speed to combine ingredients without creating a mess. Gradually increase the speed as needed.
2. **Scrape the Bowl:** Stop the mixer occasionally to scrape down the sides of the bowl with a spatula. This ensures all ingredients are fully incorporated.
3. **Avoid Overmixing:** Overmixing can lead to dense, tough baked goods. Mix just until ingredients are combined and smooth.
4. **Watch and Listen:** Pay attention to the sound and appearance of your mixture. The mixer's sound can change when ingredients are properly combined or if the motor is straining.

Understanding and mastering the settings and speeds of your KitchenAid stand mixer will transform your cooking and baking experience. Each setting has a purpose, and using them correctly will help you achieve professional-quality results right in your own kitchen.

Must-Have Accessories and Attachments

One of the greatest advantages of owning a KitchenAid stand mixer is its versatility. With a wide array of attachments and accessories, your stand mixer can do much more than just mix dough or whip cream. Let's explore some must-have accessories that can expand the functionality of your mixer and elevate your cooking and baking game.

1. Flex Edge Beater

The Flex Edge Beater is a game-changer for anyone who bakes frequently. This attachment features a flexible edge that scrapes the sides of the bowl as it mixes, ensuring all ingredients are incorporated evenly. No more stopping and scraping down the sides with a spatula—this beater does it for you, saving time and effort.

2. Dough Hook

For bread lovers, the Dough Hook is an essential attachment. It kneads dough thoroughly and efficiently, mimicking the action of hand kneading but with much less effort. Whether you're making pizza dough, artisan bread, or soft dinner rolls, the Dough Hook will ensure your dough is perfectly kneaded every time.

3. Wire Whisk

The Wire Whisk attachment is perfect for tasks that require incorporating air into your ingredients. It's ideal for whipping cream, beating egg whites, and making meringues. The whisk's design allows for maximum aeration, giving you light and fluffy results quickly.

4. Pasta Roller and Cutter Set

This attachment allows you to roll out pasta dough to your desired thickness and cut it into various shapes like fettuccine and spaghetti. Homemade pasta has never been easier, and the fresh taste is incomparable to store-bought.

5. Food Grinder

The Food Grinder attachment is perfect for grinding meats, cheese, bread crumbs, and even vegetables. It's a fantastic tool for making homemade sausages, burgers, and meatloaf. You can control the quality and texture of the grind, ensuring fresh and flavorful results.

6. Spiralizer

The Spiralizer attachment is a must-have for those who love healthy, creative meals. It turns fruits and vegetables into spirals, slices, and ribbons, perfect for making vegetable noodles, curly fries, and decorative garnishes. It's a fun way to add more veggies to your diet and impress your guests with visually appealing dishes.

7. Ice Cream Maker

Who doesn't love homemade ice cream? The Ice Cream Maker attachment lets you create your own ice cream, sorbet, and gelato right at home. Experiment with different flavors and ingredients to make custom frozen treats that are sure to delight your family and friends.

8. Grain Mill

For those who enjoy baking with freshly milled flour, the Grain Mill attachment is indispensable. It grinds grains like wheat, oats, corn, and rice into flour, allowing you to make the freshest and most flavorful baked goods.

Milling your own flour also lets you control the texture and fineness, tailoring it to your specific baking needs.

9. Food Processor

The Food Processor attachment turns your stand mixer into a powerful food processor. It slices, dices, shreds, and juliennes fruits and vegetables quickly and efficiently. This attachment is perfect for meal prep, making salads, and creating uniform slices for even cooking.

10. Citrus Juicer

The Citrus Juicer attachment makes juicing lemons, limes, oranges, and grapefruits a breeze. Freshly squeezed juice is perfect for cooking, baking, and making refreshing drinks. This attachment is easy to use and ensures you get the most juice out of every piece of fruit.

TIPS FOR USING YOUR KITCHENAID STAND MIXER

Care and Maintenance

Taking good care of your KitchenAid stand mixer is like nurturing a relationship, it pays off in the long run with consistent performance and longevity. Let's dive into some simple yet essential tips to ensure your mixer remains a trusty companion in your kitchen for years to come.

Routine Cleaning

After every use, it's important to give your stand mixer a good clean. Begin by unplugging it, safety first. Wipe down the exterior with a damp cloth to remove any splatters or spills.

For tougher spots, a bit of mild dish soap does wonders. Don't forget the bowl, attachments, and the little crevices where flour and batter love to hide.

The mixing bowl and standard attachments like the paddle, whisk, and dough hook are usually dishwasher safe, but I prefer hand washing them with warm soapy water. It's gentler and ensures they stay in tip-top shape.

Deep Cleaning

Every few months, treat your mixer to a deep clean. Remove the attachments and bowl, and wipe down the mixer's body and base thoroughly. Pay special attention to the beater shaft, where food particles can accumulate. A toothbrush or a small, soft brush works great for cleaning those tight spots.

Maintaining the Attachments

Each attachment is unique and needs a bit of TLC. For instance, the whisk has lots of little wires that can trap food. Soak it in warm soapy water before scrubbing gently. The dough hook, often dealing with sticky doughs, benefits from a quick rinse right after use to prevent residue from hardening.

Motor Maintenance

The heart of your mixer is its motor. To keep it running smoothly, avoid overloading the bowl. If a recipe calls for more than 8 cups of flour, consider mixing in batches. Listen to your mixer—if it sounds strained or is getting too hot, give it a break. Let it cool down before continuing.

Storage Tips

When your mixer isn't in use, cover it to keep dust and kitchen grease at bay. If you don't have a mixer cover, a clean kitchen towel works just as well. Store attachments and the bowl in a dry place to avoid rust and corrosion.

Troubleshooting Common Issues

Even the best mixers can face hiccups. If your mixer isn't turning on, check the power cord and outlet first. Sometimes, a simple reset is all it needs. If attachments aren't fitting properly, make sure there's no debris in the attachment hub. For persistent issues, don't hesitate to refer to your manual or reach out to KitchenAid's customer service, they're quite helpful.

Maximizing Efficiency and Performance

Proper Loading and Mixing

Start by ensuring you're using the right bowl size for your recipe. Overloading the bowl can cause the mixer to strain, leading to inconsistent results and potential motor issues. If a recipe calls for more than the standard bowl can handle, mix in batches. It's a little extra work, but it's worth it for the perfect texture.

When adding ingredients, do it gradually. Start with the dry ingredients and add the wet ingredients slowly. This helps prevent clumping and ensures an even mix. If your recipe calls for folding in delicate ingredients like whipped cream or egg whites, use the lowest speed setting or fold them in by hand to avoid overmixing.

Avoiding Common Mistakes

One common mistake is overmixing. It's easy to get carried away, especially when the mixer does all the hard work. However, overmixing can lead to dense cakes and tough cookies. Pay attention to your recipe's instructions and mix just until ingredients are combined.

Another pitfall is not scraping the bowl. Ingredients can cling to the sides and bottom of the bowl, resulting in an uneven mix. Stop the mixer occasionally to scrape down the sides with a spatula, ensuring everything gets incorporated.

Optimal Mixing Times

Each recipe is different, but as a general rule:
- **Creaming butter and sugar:** 3-5 minutes until light and fluffy.

- **Mixing cake batter:** 2-3 minutes until smooth.
- **Kneading dough:** 5-7 minutes until it forms a smooth, elastic ball.

Keeping an eye on the clock can help you avoid overmixing and achieve the perfect consistency.

Enhancing Performance with Attachments

The right attachment can significantly enhance your mixer's performance. For example, the paddle attachment is great for general mixing, while the dough hook is a must for kneading bread. The wire whisk is perfect for whipping and aerating.

Invest in attachments like the flex edge beater, which scrapes the bowl as it mixes, saving you time and effort. Consider the pasta maker or food grinder for expanding your culinary repertoire. Each attachment is designed to make specific tasks easier and more efficient.

BREADS

Classic White Bread

Prep Time: 20 minutes
Cook Time: 30-35 minutes
Servings: 1 loaf (approximately 12 slices)
Ingredients:
- 3 1/2 cups all-purpose flour
- 1 packet (2 1/4 tsp) active dry yeast
- 1 1/4 cups warm water (110°F)
- 2 tbsp granulated sugar
- 2 tbsp unsalted butter, softened
- 1 1/2 tsp salt

Instructions:
1. **Activate the Yeast:**
   - In a small bowl, combine warm water and sugar. Stir until the sugar dissolves.
   - Sprinkle the yeast over the water. Let it sit for about 5-10 minutes, or until it becomes frothy.
2. **Mix the Dough:**
   - In the bowl of your KitchenAid stand mixer, combine 3 cups of flour and salt. Attach the dough hook.
   - Add the yeast mixture and the softened butter to the flour mixture.

- Start mixing on low speed until the ingredients begin to come together. Gradually increase the speed to medium.
- Add the remaining flour, a little at a time, until the dough pulls away from the sides of the bowl and forms a ball. The dough should be smooth and elastic, not sticky.

3. **Knead the Dough:**
   - Continue to knead the dough in the mixer on medium speed for about 5-7 minutes.

4. **First Rise:**
   - Remove the dough from the bowl and shape it into a ball.
   - Place the dough in a lightly greased bowl, turning it to grease all sides.
   - Cover the bowl with a clean kitchen towel and let the dough rise in a warm, draft-free area for about 1 hour, or until it has doubled in size.

5. **Shape the Dough:**
   - Punch down the dough to release any air bubbles.
   - Turn the dough out onto a lightly floured surface and shape it into a loaf.
   - Place the shaped dough into a greased 9x5-inch loaf pan.

6. **Second Rise:**

- Cover the loaf pan with a kitchen towel and let the dough rise for about 30-40 minutes, or until it has doubled in size again.
7. **Bake the Bread:**
   - Preheat your oven to 375°F (190°C).
   - Bake the bread for 30-35 minutes, or until the top is golden brown and the loaf sounds hollow when tapped.
   - If the top is browning too quickly, cover it with a piece of aluminum foil.
8. **Cool the Bread:**
   - Remove the loaf from the oven and let it cool in the pan for about 10 minutes.
   - Transfer the bread to a wire rack to cool completely before slicing.

Nutritional Information (per slice):
- Calories: 150
- Carbohydrates: 28g
- Protein: 4g
- Fat: 2g
- Fiber: 1g
- Sugar: 2g
- Sodium: 200mg

Tips:
- Ensure your water is the right temperature (110°F) to activate the yeast properly.
- If you prefer a softer crust, brush the top of the loaf with melted butter immediately after baking.
- Store the bread in a bread box or wrap it in a cloth to keep it fresh for several days. You can also freeze the bread for up to 3 months.

Whole Wheat Bread

Prep Time: 20 minutes
Cook Time: 30-35 minutes
Servings: 1 loaf (approximately 12 slices)
Ingredients:
- 3 1/2 cups whole wheat flour
- 1 packet (2 1/4 tsp) active dry yeast
- 1 1/4 cups warm water (110°F)
- 2 tbsp honey
- 2 tbsp unsalted butter, softened
- 1 1/2 tsp salt
- 1/4 cup dry milk powder (optional for a softer texture)

Instructions:
1. **Activate the Yeast:**
   o In a small bowl, combine warm water and honey. Stir until the honey dissolves.
   o Sprinkle the yeast over the water. Let it sit for about 5-10 minutes, or until it becomes frothy.
2. **Mix the Dough:**
   o In the bowl of your KitchenAid stand mixer, combine 3 cups of whole wheat flour, salt, and dry milk powder (if using). Attach the dough hook.
   o Add the yeast mixture and the softened butter to the flour mixture.

- Start mixing on low speed until the ingredients begin to come together. Gradually increase the speed to medium.
- Add the remaining flour, a little at a time, until the dough pulls away from the sides of the bowl and forms a ball. The dough should be smooth and elastic, not sticky.

3. **Knead the Dough:**
   - Continue to knead the dough in the mixer on medium speed for about 5-7 minutes.

4. **First Rise:**
   - Remove the dough from the bowl and shape it into a ball.
   - Place the dough in a lightly greased bowl, turning it to grease all sides.
   - Cover the bowl with a clean kitchen towel and let the dough rise in a warm, draft-free area for about 1 hour, or until it has doubled in size.

5. **Shape the Dough:**
   - Punch down the dough to release any air bubbles.
   - Turn the dough out onto a lightly floured surface and shape it into a loaf.
   - Place the shaped dough into a greased 9x5-inch loaf pan.

6. **Second Rise:**

- o Cover the loaf pan with a kitchen towel and let the dough rise for about 30-40 minutes, or until it has doubled in size again.
7. **Bake the Bread:**
   - o Preheat your oven to 375°F (190°C).
   - o Bake the bread for 30-35 minutes, or until the top is golden brown and the loaf sounds hollow when tapped.
   - o If the top is browning too quickly, cover it with a piece of aluminum foil.
8. **Cool the Bread:**
   - o Remove the loaf from the oven and let it cool in the pan for about 10 minutes.
   - o Transfer the bread to a wire rack to cool completely before slicing.

Nutritional Information (per slice):
- Calories: 140
- Carbohydrates: 26g
- Protein: 4g
- Fat: 2g
- Fiber: 4g
- Sugar: 3g
- Sodium: 200mg

Tips:
- Whole wheat flour absorbs more liquid than white flour, so adjust the water if needed.
- Adding dry milk powder helps create a softer texture and enhances the nutritional value.

Multigrain Bread

Prep Time: 25 minutes
Cook Time: 35-40 minutes
Servings: 1 loaf (approximately 12 slices)
Ingredients:

- 2 cups whole wheat flour
- 1 cup bread flour
- 1/2 cup rolled oats
- 1/4 cup sunflower seeds
- 1/4 cup flaxseeds
- 1/4 cup millet
- 1 packet (2 1/4 tsp) active dry yeast
- 1 1/4 cups warm water (110°F)
- 2 tbsp honey
- 2 tbsp unsalted butter, softened
- 1 1/2 tsp salt

Instructions:

1. **Activate the Yeast:**
   - In a small bowl, combine warm water and honey. Stir until the honey dissolves.
   - Sprinkle the yeast over the water. Let it sit for about 5-10 minutes, or until it becomes frothy.
2. **Mix the Dough:**
   - In the bowl of your KitchenAid stand mixer, combine whole wheat flour, bread flour, rolled oats, sunflower seeds, flaxseeds, millet, and salt. Attach the dough hook.

- Add the yeast mixture and the softened butter to the flour mixture.
- Start mixing on low speed until the ingredients begin to come together. Gradually increase the speed to medium.
- Add more water or flour if needed until the dough pulls away from the sides of the bowl and forms a ball. The dough should be smooth and elastic, not sticky.

3. **Knead the Dough:**
   - Continue to knead the dough in the mixer on medium speed for about 5-7 minutes.

4. **First Rise:**
   - Remove the dough from the bowl and shape it into a ball.
   - Place the dough in a lightly greased bowl, turning it to grease all sides.
   - Cover the bowl with a clean kitchen towel and let the dough rise in a warm, draft-free area for about 1 hour, or until it has doubled in size.

5. **Shape the Dough:**
   - Punch down the dough to release any air bubbles.
   - Turn the dough out onto a lightly floured surface and shape it into a loaf.
   - Place the shaped dough into a greased 9x5-inch loaf pan.

6. **Second Rise:**

- Cover the loaf pan with a kitchen towel and let the dough rise for about 30-40 minutes, or until it has doubled in size again.

7. **Bake the Bread:**
   - Preheat your oven to 375°F (190°C).
   - Bake the bread for 35-40 minutes, or until the top is golden brown and the loaf sounds hollow when tapped.
   - If the top is browning too quickly, cover it with a piece of aluminum foil.

8. **Cool the Bread:**
   - Remove the loaf from the oven and let it cool in the pan for about 10 minutes.
   - Transfer the bread to a wire rack to cool completely before slicing.

Nutritional Information (per slice):
- Calories: 160
- Carbohydrates: 28g
- Protein: 5g
- Fat: 4g
- Fiber: 5g
- Sugar: 3g
- Sodium: 200mg

Tips:
- Experiment with different seeds and grains to customize your multigrain bread.
- Adding a bit of honey or molasses can enhance the flavor and help with browning.

Sourdough Bread

Prep Time: 20 minutes (plus 12-18 hours fermentation time)
Cook Time: 40-45 minutes
Servings: 1 loaf (approximately 12 slices)
Ingredients:
- 3 1/2 cups bread flour
- 1 1/2 cups sourdough starter (fed and active)
- 1 cup water
- 2 tsp salt

Instructions:
1. **Mix the Dough:**
   o In the bowl of your KitchenAid stand mixer, combine the bread flour and salt. Attach the dough hook.
   o Add the sourdough starter and water to the flour mixture.
   o Start mixing on low speed until the ingredients begin to come together. Gradually increase the speed to medium.
   o Mix until the dough pulls away from the sides of the bowl and forms a ball. The dough should be smooth and elastic, not sticky.
2. **Autolyse:**
   o Cover the bowl with a damp kitchen towel and let the dough rest for 30 minutes. This

allows the flour to hydrate and the gluten to develop.

3. **Knead the Dough:**
   - After the autolyse, knead the dough in the mixer on medium speed for about 5-7 minutes.

4. **Bulk Fermentation:**
   - Transfer the dough to a lightly greased bowl. Cover it with a damp kitchen towel.
   - Let the dough ferment at room temperature for 12-18 hours, or until it has doubled in size. The longer the fermentation, the better the flavor.

5. **Shape the Dough:**
   - Turn the dough out onto a lightly floured surface. Gently shape it into a round or oval loaf.
   - Place the shaped dough into a greased or parchment-lined Dutch oven or a proofing basket.

6. **Second Rise:**
   - Cover the dough with a kitchen towel and let it rise for about 2 hours, or until it has doubled in size.

7. **Bake the Bread:**
   - Preheat your oven to 450°F (230°C). If using a Dutch oven, place it in the oven to preheat as well.
   - Score the top of the loaf with a sharp knife.

- o If using a Dutch oven, carefully place the dough into the preheated pot, cover it with the lid, and bake for 20 minutes. Remove the lid and bake for an additional 20-25 minutes, or until the crust is deeply golden and the loaf sounds hollow when tapped.
- o If not using a Dutch oven, bake the loaf on a baking sheet with a pan of water in the bottom of the oven for steam.

8. **Cool the Bread:**
  - o Remove the bread from the oven and let it cool completely on a wire rack before slicing.

Nutritional Information (per slice):
- Calories: 150
- Carbohydrates: 30g
- Protein: 4g
- Fat: 0g
- Fiber: 2g
- Sugar: 0g
- Sodium: 300mg

Tips:
- Sourdough starter should be fed and bubbly before using it in the recipe.
- For a crispier crust, let the bread cool completely in the oven with the door slightly ajar.

Rye Bread

Prep Time: 20 minutes
Cook Time: 35-40 minutes
Servings: 1 loaf (approximately 12 slices)

Ingredients:

- 2 cups rye flour
- 1 1/2 cups bread flour
- 1 packet (2 1/4 tsp) active dry yeast
- 1 1/4 cups warm water (110°F)
- 2 tbsp molasses
- 2 tbsp unsalted butter, softened
- 1 1/2 tsp salt
- 1 tbsp caraway seeds (optional)

Instructions:

1. **Activate the Yeast:**
   - In a small bowl, combine warm water and molasses. Stir until the molasses dissolves.
   - Sprinkle the yeast over the water. Let it sit for about 5-10 minutes, or until it becomes frothy.

2. **Mix the Dough:**
   - In the bowl of your KitchenAid stand mixer, combine rye flour, bread flour, salt, and caraway seeds (if using). Attach the dough hook.
   - Add the yeast mixture and the softened butter to the flour mixture.

- Start mixing on low speed until the ingredients begin to come together. Gradually increase the speed to medium.
- Mix until the dough pulls away from the sides of the bowl and forms a ball. The dough should be smooth and elastic, not sticky.

3. **Knead the Dough:**
   - Continue to knead the dough in the mixer on medium speed for about 5-7 minutes.

4. **First Rise:**
   - Remove the dough from the bowl and shape it into a ball.
   - Place the dough in a lightly greased bowl, turning it to grease all sides.
   - Cover the bowl with a clean kitchen towel and let the dough rise in a warm, draft-free area for about 1 hour, or until it has doubled in size.

5. **Shape the Dough:**
   - Punch down the dough to release any air bubbles.
   - Turn the dough out onto a lightly floured surface and shape it into a loaf.
   - Place the shaped dough into a greased 9x5-inch loaf pan.

6. **Second Rise:**

- o Cover the loaf pan with a kitchen towel and let the dough rise for about 30-40 minutes, or until it has doubled in size again.
7. **Bake the Bread:**
   - o Preheat your oven to 375°F (190°C).
   - o Bake the bread for 35-40 minutes, or until the top is golden brown and the loaf sounds hollow when tapped.
   - o If the top is browning too quickly, cover it with a piece of aluminum foil.
8. **Cool the Bread:**
   - o Remove the loaf from the oven and let it cool in the pan for about 10 minutes.
   - o Transfer the bread to a wire rack to cool completely before slicing.

Nutritional Information (per slice):
- Calories: 160
- Carbohydrates: 28g
- Protein: 5g
- Fat: 2g
- Fiber: 4g
- Sugar: 2g
- Sodium: 200mg

Tips:
- Using molasses gives the rye bread its characteristic deep flavor and color.
- Caraway seeds are optional but add a traditional taste to rye bread.
- Ensure the water is the right temperature to properly activate the yeast.

Ciabatta

Prep Time: 25 minutes (plus 2 hours rising time)
Cook Time: 20-25 minutes
Servings: 2 loaves

Ingredients:
- 4 cups all-purpose flour
- 1 packet (2 1/4 tsp) active dry yeast
- 2 cups warm water (110°F)
- 2 tbsp olive oil
- 2 tsp salt

Instructions:
1. **Activate the Yeast:**
   - In a small bowl, combine warm water and yeast. Let it sit for about 5-10 minutes, or until it becomes frothy.
2. **Mix the Dough:**
   - In the bowl of your KitchenAid stand mixer, combine the flour and salt. Attach the dough hook.
   - Add the yeast mixture and olive oil to the flour mixture.
   - Start mixing on low speed until the ingredients begin to come together. Gradually increase the speed to medium.
   - Mix until the dough is smooth and elastic. It will be very sticky, which is normal for ciabatta dough.
3. **First Rise:**

- Transfer the dough to a lightly greased bowl. Cover it with a clean kitchen towel.
- Let it rise in a warm, draft-free area for about 1 hour, or until it has doubled in size.

4. **Shape the Dough:**
   - Turn the dough out onto a well-floured surface. Divide it into two pieces.
   - Shape each piece into a rough oval and place them on a parchment-lined baking sheet. Handle the dough gently to keep the air bubbles intact.

5. **Second Rise:**
   - Cover the loaves with a kitchen towel and let them rise for about 1 hour.

6. **Bake the Bread:**
   - Preheat your oven to 425°F (220°C).
   - Bake the loaves for 20-25 minutes, or until they are golden brown and sound hollow when tapped.
   - For a crispier crust, you can spray water into the oven a few times during the first 10 minutes of baking.

7. **Cool the Bread:**
   - Remove the loaves from the oven and let them cool on a wire rack before slicing.

Nutritional Information (per slice):
- Calories: 150
- Carbohydrates: 30g
- Protein: 5g

- Fat: 2g
- Fiber: 1g
- Sugar: 0g
- Sodium: 300mg

Tips:

- The dough for ciabatta is very wet and sticky, which helps create the large air pockets characteristic of this bread.
- Using a high-quality olive oil can enhance the flavor of the bread.
- Be gentle when shaping the dough to preserve its airy structure.

Focaccia

Prep Time: 20 minutes (plus 2 hours rising time)
Cook Time: 25-30 minutes
Servings: 1 large focaccia (approximately 16 slices)
Ingredients:
- 4 cups all-purpose flour
- 1 packet (2 1/4 tsp) active dry yeast
- 1 1/2 cups warm water (110°F)
- 1/4 cup olive oil (plus extra for drizzling)
- 2 tsp salt
- 1 tbsp sugar
- Fresh rosemary, sea salt, and cherry tomatoes for topping (optional)

Instructions:
1. **Activate the Yeast:**
   o In a small bowl, combine warm water, sugar, and yeast. Let it sit for about 5-10 minutes, or until it becomes frothy.
2. **Mix the Dough:**
   o In the bowl of your KitchenAid stand mixer, combine the flour and salt. Attach the dough hook.
   o Add the yeast mixture and 1/4 cup olive oil to the flour mixture.
   o Start mixing on low speed until the ingredients begin to come together. Gradually increase the speed to medium.
   o Mix until the dough is smooth and elastic.

3. **First Rise:**
   - Transfer the dough to a lightly greased bowl. Cover it with a clean kitchen towel.
   - Let it rise in a warm, draft-free area for about 1 hour, or until it has doubled in size.
4. **Shape the Dough:**
   - Turn the dough out onto a lightly floured surface. Gently press it into a large, rectangular shape about 1/2 inch thick.
   - Transfer the dough to a greased baking sheet.
5. **Second Rise:**
   - Cover the dough with a kitchen towel and let it rise for about 1 hour.
6. **Prepare for Baking:**
   - Preheat your oven to 400°F (200°C).
   - Use your fingers to make dimples all over the surface of the dough.
   - Drizzle with olive oil and sprinkle with fresh rosemary, sea salt, and cherry tomatoes if desired.
7. **Bake the Bread:**
   - Bake for 25-30 minutes, or until the focaccia is golden brown and sounds hollow when tapped.
8. **Cool the Bread:**
   - Remove the focaccia from the oven and let it cool on a wire rack before slicing.

Nutritional Information (per slice):

- Calories: 180
- Carbohydrates: 30g
- Protein: 5g
- Fat: 5g
- Fiber: 1g
- Sugar: 1g
- Sodium: 350mg

Tips:

- For a crispier bottom, bake the focaccia on a preheated baking stone.
- Experiment with different toppings such as olives, onions, or different herbs.
- Ensure the dough has plenty of olive oil to achieve a rich, flavorful crust.

Brioche

Prep Time: 30 minutes (plus 2 hours rising time)
Cook Time: 35-40 minutes
Servings: 1 loaf (approximately 12 slices)
Ingredients:
- 4 cups all-purpose flour
- 1/4 cup granulated sugar
- 1 packet (2 1/4 tsp) active dry yeast
- 1/2 cup warm milk (110°F)
- 5 large eggs (4 for the dough, 1 for egg wash)
- 1 tsp salt
- 1 cup unsalted butter, softened

Instructions:
1. **Activate the Yeast:**
    - In a small bowl, combine warm milk and sugar. Stir until the sugar dissolves.
    - Sprinkle the yeast over the milk. Let it sit for about 5-10 minutes, or until it becomes frothy.
2. **Mix the Dough:**
    - In the bowl of your KitchenAid stand mixer, combine the flour and salt. Attach the dough hook.
    - Add the yeast mixture and 4 eggs to the flour mixture.
    - Start mixing on low speed until the ingredients begin to come together. Gradually increase the speed to medium.

3. **Add Butter:**
   - Gradually add the softened butter to the dough, a few tablespoons at a time, while continuing to mix.
   - Mix until the dough is smooth, glossy, and elastic. This may take about 10-15 minutes.
4. **First Rise:**
   - Transfer the dough to a lightly greased bowl. Cover it with a clean kitchen towel.
   - Let it rise in a warm, draft-free area for about 1 hour, or until it has doubled in size.
5. **Shape the Dough:**
   - Punch down the dough to release any air bubbles.
   - Turn the dough out onto a lightly floured surface. Divide it into three equal pieces and roll each piece into a rope.
   - Braid the ropes together and place them in a greased 9x5-inch loaf pan.
6. **Second Rise:**
   - Cover the loaf pan with a kitchen towel and let the dough rise for about 1 hour, or until it has doubled in size.
7. **Prepare for Baking:**
   - Preheat your oven to 375°F (190°C).
   - Beat the remaining egg and brush it over the top of the loaf.
8. **Bake the Bread:**

- Bake for 35-40 minutes, or until the top is golden brown and the loaf sounds hollow when tapped.
- If the top is browning too quickly, cover it with a piece of aluminum foil.

9. **Cool the Bread:**
   - Remove the loaf from the oven and let it cool in the pan for about 10 minutes.
   - Transfer the bread to a wire rack to cool completely before slicing.

Nutritional Information (per slice):
- Calories: 240
- Carbohydrates: 28g
- Protein: 6g
- Fat: 12g
- Fiber: 1g
- Sugar: 6g
- Sodium: 200mg

Tips:
- Brioche dough is very rich and buttery; ensure all ingredients are at room temperature for best results.
- If you prefer a sweeter brioche, increase the sugar to 1/2 cup.
- For a savory twist, add herbs or cheese to the dough before braiding.

Bagels

Prep Time: 45 minutes (plus 1 hour rising time)
Cook Time: 20-25 minutes
Servings: 12 bagels
Ingredients:
- 4 cups bread flour
- 1 packet (2 1/4 tsp) active dry yeast
- 1 1/2 cups warm water (110°F)
- 2 tbsp granulated sugar
- 1 tbsp barley malt syrup or honey
- 2 tsp salt
- 1 egg white (for egg wash)
- Toppings: sesame seeds, poppy seeds, everything bagel seasoning (optional)

Instructions:
1. **Activate the Yeast:**
   - In a small bowl, combine warm water and sugar. Stir until the sugar dissolves.
   - Sprinkle the yeast over the water. Let it sit for about 5-10 minutes, or until it becomes frothy.
2. **Mix the Dough:**
   - In the bowl of your KitchenAid stand mixer, combine the flour and salt. Attach the dough hook.
   - Add the yeast mixture and barley malt syrup (or honey) to the flour mixture.

- Start mixing on low speed until the ingredients begin to come together. Gradually increase the speed to medium.
- Mix until the dough is smooth and elastic, about 7-10 minutes.

3. **First Rise:**
   - Transfer the dough to a lightly greased bowl. Cover it with a clean kitchen towel.
   - Let it rise in a warm, draft-free area for about 1 hour, or until it has doubled in size.

4. **Shape the Bagels:**
   - Punch down the dough to release any air bubbles.
   - Turn the dough out onto a lightly floured surface and divide it into 12 equal pieces.
   - Roll each piece into a ball, then use your thumb to poke a hole in the center and stretch it to form a ring.

5. **Boil the Bagels:**
   - Preheat your oven to 425°F (220°C).
   - Bring a large pot of water to a boil. Reduce the heat to a simmer and add the bagels, a few at a time, boiling each for about 1 minute per side.
   - Remove the bagels with a slotted spoon and place them on a parchment-lined baking sheet.

6. **Prepare for Baking:**

- o Beat the egg white and brush it over the tops of the bagels.
- o Sprinkle with your desired toppings.
7. **Bake the Bagels:**
    - o Bake for 20-25 minutes, or until the bagels are golden brown and sound hollow when tapped.
8. **Cool the Bagels:**
    - o Remove the bagels from the oven and let them cool on a wire rack.

Nutritional Information (per bagel):
- Calories: 250
- Carbohydrates: 50g
- Protein: 8g
- Fat: 1g
- Fiber: 2g
- Sugar: 4g
- Sodium: 350mg

Tips:
- Ensure the water is at the right temperature to activate the yeast properly.
- For a chewier texture, you can add 1 tablespoon of baking soda to the boiling water.
- Store the bagels in an airtight container for up to 3 days.

English Muffins

Prep Time: 20 minutes (plus 1 hour rising time)
Cook Time: 15-20 minutes
Servings: 12 muffins
Ingredients:
- 4 cups all-purpose flour
- 1 packet (2 1/4 tsp) active dry yeast
- 1 1/2 cups warm milk (110°F)
- 2 tbsp granulated sugar
- 1/4 cup unsalted butter, melted
- 1 tsp salt
- Cornmeal for dusting

Instructions:
1. **Activate the Yeast:**
   - In a small bowl, combine warm milk and sugar. Stir until the sugar dissolves.
   - Sprinkle the yeast over the milk. Let it sit for about 5-10 minutes, or until it becomes frothy.
2. **Mix the Dough:**
   - In the bowl of your KitchenAid stand mixer, combine the flour and salt. Attach the dough hook.
   - Add the yeast mixture and melted butter to the flour mixture.
   - Start mixing on low speed until the ingredients begin to come together. Gradually increase the speed to medium.

- o Mix until the dough is smooth and elastic, about 7-10 minutes.
3. **First Rise:**
    - o Transfer the dough to a lightly greased bowl. Cover it with a clean kitchen towel.
    - o Let it rise in a warm, draft-free area for about 1 hour, or until it has doubled in size.
4. **Shape the Muffins:**
    - o Punch down the dough to release any air bubbles.
    - o Turn the dough out onto a lightly floured surface and roll it out to about 1/2 inch thickness.
    - o Use a round cutter to cut out muffins and place them on a baking sheet dusted with cornmeal.
    - o Sprinkle the tops with more cornmeal and cover with a kitchen towel. Let them rise for about 30 minutes.
5. **Cook the Muffins:**
    - o Preheat a griddle or large skillet over medium heat.
    - o Cook the muffins for about 7-10 minutes per side, or until they are golden brown and cooked through.
6. **Cool the Muffins:**
    - o Remove the muffins from the griddle and let them cool on a wire rack.

Nutritional Information (per muffin):
- Calories: 180
- Carbohydrates: 30g
- Protein: 5g
- Fat: 4g
- Fiber: 1g
- Sugar: 3g
- Sodium: 200mg

Tips:
- Ensure the milk is at the right temperature to activate the yeast properly.
- For best results, use a thermometer to ensure the internal temperature of the muffins reaches 200°F.
- English muffins are best when toasted before serving.

COOKIES

Chocolate Chip Cookies

Prep Time: 15 minutes
Cook Time: 10-12 minutes
Servings: 24 cookies

Ingredients:

- 2 1/4 cups all-purpose flour
- 1 tsp baking soda
- 1/2 tsp salt
- 1 cup unsalted butter, softened
- 3/4 cup granulated sugar
- 3/4 cup packed brown sugar
- 1 tsp vanilla extract
- 2 large eggs
- 2 cups semi-sweet chocolate chips

Instructions:

1. **Preheat the Oven:**
   - Preheat your oven to 375°F (190°C). Line two baking sheets with parchment paper.
2. **Mix Dry Ingredients:**
   - In a medium bowl, whisk together the flour, baking soda, and salt.
3. **Cream Butter and Sugars:**
   - In the bowl of your KitchenAid stand mixer, beat the butter, granulated sugar, brown

sugar, and vanilla extract on medium speed until creamy.

4. **Add Eggs:**
   - Add the eggs, one at a time, beating well after each addition.

5. **Combine Wet and Dry Ingredients:**
   - Gradually add the flour mixture to the butter mixture, mixing on low speed until combined.

6. **Add Chocolate Chips:**
   - Stir in the chocolate chips until evenly distributed.

7. **Shape the Cookies:**
   - Drop rounded tablespoonfuls of dough onto the prepared baking sheets, spacing them about 2 inches apart.

8. **Bake the Cookies:**
   - Bake for 10-12 minutes, or until the edges are golden brown but the centers are still soft.
   - Remove from the oven and let the cookies cool on the baking sheets for 2 minutes, then transfer to wire racks to cool completely.

Nutritional Information (per cookie):
- Calories: 200
- Carbohydrates: 28g
- Protein: 2g
- Fat: 10g
- Fiber: 1g

- Sugar: 18g
- Sodium: 150mg

Tips:

- For chewier cookies, chill the dough for 30 minutes before baking.
- Use a combination of semi-sweet and milk chocolate chips for a richer flavor.
- Store the cookies in an airtight container to keep them fresh.

Oatmeal Raisin Cookies

Prep Time: 15 minutes
Cook Time: 10-12 minutes
Servings: 24 cookies

Ingredients:
- 1 1/2 cups all-purpose flour
- 1 tsp baking soda
- 1 tsp ground cinnamon
- 1/2 tsp salt
- 1 cup unsalted butter, softened
- 3/4 cup granulated sugar
- 3/4 cup packed brown sugar
- 2 large eggs
- 1 tsp vanilla extract
- 3 cups old-fashioned oats
- 1 cup raisins

Instructions:
1. **Preheat the Oven:**
   o Preheat your oven to 350°F (175°C). Line two baking sheets with parchment paper.
2. **Mix Dry Ingredients:**
   o In a medium bowl, whisk together the flour, baking soda, cinnamon, and salt.
3. **Cream Butter and Sugars:**
   o In the bowl of your KitchenAid stand mixer, beat the butter, granulated sugar, and brown sugar on medium speed until creamy.
4. **Add Eggs:**

o   Add the eggs, one at a time, beating well
    after each addition. Stir in the vanilla
    extract.

5. **Combine Wet and Dry Ingredients:**
    o   Gradually add the flour mixture to the butter
        mixture, mixing on low speed until
        combined.

6. **Add Oats and Raisins:**
    o   Stir in the oats and raisins until evenly
        distributed.

7. **Shape the Cookies:**
    o   Drop rounded tablespoonfuls of dough onto
        the prepared baking sheets, spacing them
        about 2 inches apart.

8. **Bake the Cookies:**
    o   Bake for 10-12 minutes, or until the edges
        are golden brown but the centers are still
        soft.
    o   Remove from the oven and let the cookies
        cool on the baking sheets for 2 minutes, then
        transfer to wire racks to cool completely.

Nutritional Information (per cookie):
- Calories: 180
- Carbohydrates: 28g
- Protein: 3g
- Fat: 7g
- Fiber: 2g
- Sugar: 15g
- Sodium: 150mg

Tips:
- For a twist, add 1/2 cup of chopped nuts or chocolate chips to the dough.
- Ensure the butter is at room temperature for easier creaming.
- Use fresh, plump raisins for the best flavor and texture.

Peanut Butter Cookies

Prep Time: 15 minutes
Cook Time: 10-12 minutes
Servings: 24 cookies
Ingredients:
- 1 1/4 cups all-purpose flour
- 1/2 tsp baking soda
- 1/2 tsp baking powder
- 1/4 tsp salt
- 1/2 cup unsalted butter, softened
- 1/2 cup granulated sugar
- 1/2 cup packed brown sugar
- 1 cup creamy peanut butter
- 1 large egg
- 1 tsp vanilla extract

Instructions:
1. **Preheat the Oven:**
   - Preheat your oven to 350°F (175°C). Line two baking sheets with parchment paper.
2. **Mix Dry Ingredients:**
   - In a medium bowl, whisk together the flour, baking soda, baking powder, and salt.
3. **Cream Butter and Sugars:**
   - In the bowl of your KitchenAid stand mixer, beat the butter, granulated sugar, brown sugar, and peanut butter on medium speed until creamy.
4. **Add Egg and Vanilla:**
   - Add the egg and vanilla extract, beating well until combined.

5. **Combine Wet and Dry Ingredients:**
   o Gradually add the flour mixture to the butter mixture, mixing on low speed until combined.
6. **Shape the Cookies:**
   o Roll tablespoonfuls of dough into balls and place them on the prepared baking sheets.
   o Flatten each ball with a fork, making a crisscross pattern.
7. **Bake the Cookies:**
   o Bake for 10-12 minutes, or until the edges are golden brown.
   o Remove from the oven and let the cookies cool on the baking sheets for 2 minutes, then transfer to wire racks to cool completely.

Nutritional Information (per cookie):
- Calories: 170
- Carbohydrates: 18g
- Protein: 4g
- Fat: 10g
- Fiber: 1g
- Sugar: 12g
- Sodium: 150mg

Tips:
- For a chewier texture, use brown sugar only.
- Add 1/2 cup of chocolate chips or chopped peanuts for extra flavor.
- Ensure the cookies are slightly underbaked for a softer center.

Snickerdoodles

Prep Time: 15 minutes
Cook Time: 10-12 minutes
Servings: 24 cookies
Ingredients:
- 2 3/4 cups all-purpose flour
- 2 tsp cream of tartar
- 1 tsp baking soda
- 1/2 tsp salt
- 1 cup unsalted butter, softened
- 1 1/2 cups granulated sugar
- 2 large eggs
- 1 tsp vanilla extract
- 2 tbsp granulated sugar (for rolling)
- 1 tbsp ground cinnamon (for rolling)

Instructions:
1. **Preheat the Oven:**
   o Preheat your oven to 375°F (190°C). Line two baking sheets with parchment paper.
2. **Mix Dry Ingredients:**
   o In a medium bowl, whisk together the flour, cream of tartar, baking soda, and salt.
3. **Cream Butter and Sugar:**
   o In the bowl of your KitchenAid stand mixer, beat the butter and 1 1/2 cups of granulated sugar on medium speed until creamy.
4. **Add Eggs and Vanilla:**

o   Add the eggs, one at a time, beating well after each addition. Stir in the vanilla extract.

5. **Combine Wet and Dry Ingredients:**
   o   Gradually add the flour mixture to the butter mixture, mixing on low speed until combined.

6. **Prepare the Rolling Mixture:**
   o   In a small bowl, combine 2 tablespoons of granulated sugar and 1 tablespoon of ground cinnamon.

7. **Shape the Cookies:**
   o   Roll tablespoonfuls of dough into balls and roll each ball in the cinnamon-sugar mixture.
   o   Place the dough balls on the prepared baking sheets, spacing them about 2 inches apart.

8. **Bake the Cookies:**
   o   Bake for 10-12 minutes, or until the edges are set and the centers are soft.
   o   Remove from the oven and let the cookies cool on the baking sheets for 2 minutes, then transfer to wire racks to cool completely.

Nutritional Information (per cookie):
- Calories: 160
- Carbohydrates: 22g
- Protein: 2g
- Fat: 7g
- Fiber: 0g

- Sugar: 14g
- Sodium: 90mg

Tips:

- For a softer cookie, slightly underbake the cookies.
- If you prefer a stronger cinnamon flavor, increase the amount of cinnamon in the rolling mixture.
- Store the cookies in an airtight container to keep them soft.

Sugar Cookies

Prep Time: 15 minutes (plus 1 hour chilling time)
Cook Time: 8-10 minutes
Servings: 24 cookies

Ingredients:

- 2 3/4 cups all-purpose flour
- 1 tsp baking soda
- 1/2 tsp baking powder
- 1/2 tsp salt
- 1 cup unsalted butter, softened
- 1 1/2 cups granulated sugar
- 1 large egg
- 1 tsp vanilla extract
- 1/2 tsp almond extract (optional)
- Colored sugar or sprinkles (optional, for decorating)

Instructions:

1. **Mix Dry Ingredients:**
   - In a medium bowl, whisk together the flour, baking soda, baking powder, and salt.
2. **Cream Butter and Sugar:**
   - In the bowl of your KitchenAid stand mixer, beat the butter and granulated sugar on medium speed until creamy.
3. **Add Egg and Extracts:**
   - Add the egg, vanilla extract, and almond extract (if using), beating well until combined.
4. **Combine Wet and Dry Ingredients:**

o   Gradually add the flour mixture to the butter mixture, mixing on low speed until combined.

5. **Chill the Dough:**
   o   Cover the dough with plastic wrap and refrigerate for at least 1 hour.

6. **Preheat the Oven:**
   o   Preheat your oven to 350°F (175°C). Line two baking sheets with parchment paper.

7. **Shape the Cookies:**
   o   Roll tablespoonfuls of dough into balls and place them on the prepared baking sheets.
   o   Flatten each ball slightly with the bottom of a glass dipped in sugar or decorate with colored sugar or sprinkles if desired.

8. **Bake the Cookies:**
   o   Bake for 8-10 minutes, or until the edges are set and the centers are soft.
   o   Remove from the oven and let the cookies cool on the baking sheets for 2 minutes, then transfer to wire racks to cool completely.

Nutritional Information (per cookie):
- Calories: 160
- Carbohydrates: 22g
- Protein: 2g
- Fat: 7g
- Fiber: 0g
- Sugar: 14g

- Sodium: 90mg

Tips:
- For a crispier cookie, bake for an additional 1-2 minutes.
- Chill the dough well to prevent the cookies from spreading too much during baking.
- These cookies are perfect for decorating with icing or sprinkles for special occasions.

Double Chocolate Cookies

Prep Time: 15 minutes
Cook Time: 10-12 minutes
Servings: 24 cookies
Ingredients:
- 1 cup all-purpose flour
- 1/2 cup unsweetened cocoa powder
- 1 tsp baking soda
- 1/2 tsp salt
- 1/2 cup unsalted butter, softened
- 1/2 cup granulated sugar
- 1/2 cup packed brown sugar
- 1 large egg
- 1 tsp vanilla extract
- 1 cup semi-sweet chocolate chips

Instructions:
1. **Preheat the Oven:**
   o Preheat your oven to 350°F (175°C). Line two baking sheets with parchment paper.
2. **Mix Dry Ingredients:**
   o In a medium bowl, whisk together the flour, cocoa powder, baking soda, and salt.
3. **Cream Butter and Sugars:**
   o In the bowl of your KitchenAid stand mixer, beat the butter, granulated sugar, and brown sugar on medium speed until creamy.

4. **Add Egg and Vanilla:**
   - Add the egg and vanilla extract, beating well until combined.
5. **Combine Wet and Dry Ingredients:**
   - Gradually add the flour mixture to the butter mixture, mixing on low speed until combined.
6. **Add Chocolate Chips:**
   - Stir in the chocolate chips until evenly distributed.
7. **Shape the Cookies:**
   - Drop rounded tablespoonfuls of dough onto the prepared baking sheets, spacing them about 2 inches apart.
8. **Bake the Cookies:**
   - Bake for 10-12 minutes, or until the edges are set and the centers are soft.
   - Remove from the oven and let the cookies cool on the baking sheets for 2 minutes, then transfer to wire racks to cool completely.

Nutritional Information (per cookie):
- Calories: 170
- Carbohydrates: 24g
- Protein: 2g
- Fat: 8g
- Fiber: 1g
- Sugar: 15g
- Sodium: 90mg

Tips:

- For an extra chocolatey flavor, use dark chocolate chips or chunks.
- Slightly underbake the cookies for a fudgier texture.
- Store the cookies in an airtight container to keep them fresh and soft.

Gingerbread Cookies

Prep Time: 20 minutes (plus 1 hour chilling time)
Cook Time: 8-10 minutes
Servings: 24 cookies
Ingredients:
- 3 cups all-purpose flour
- 3/4 cup packed brown sugar
- 1 tbsp ground ginger
- 1 tbsp ground cinnamon
- 1/2 tsp ground cloves
- 1/2 tsp ground nutmeg
- 1/2 tsp baking soda
- 1/2 tsp salt
- 3/4 cup unsalted butter, softened
- 3/4 cup molasses
- 1 large egg

Instructions:
1. **Mix Dry Ingredients:**
   o In a medium bowl, whisk together the flour, brown sugar, ginger, cinnamon, cloves, nutmeg, baking soda, and salt.
2. **Cream Butter and Molasses:**
   o In the bowl of your KitchenAid stand mixer, beat the butter and molasses on medium speed until creamy.
3. **Add Egg:**
   o Add the egg, beating well until combined.

4. **Combine Wet and Dry Ingredients:**
   - ○ Gradually add the flour mixture to the butter mixture, mixing on low speed until combined.
5. **Chill the Dough:**
   - ○ Divide the dough into two discs, wrap each in plastic wrap, and refrigerate for at least 1 hour.
6. **Preheat the Oven:**
   - ○ Preheat your oven to 350°F (175°C). Line two baking sheets with parchment paper.
7. **Shape the Cookies:**
   - ○ Roll out the dough on a lightly floured surface to 1/4-inch thickness.
   - ○ Cut into desired shapes with cookie cutters and place on the prepared baking sheets.
8. **Bake the Cookies:**
   - ○ Bake for 8-10 minutes, or until the edges are set.
   - ○ Remove from the oven and let the cookies cool on the baking sheets for 2 minutes, then transfer to wire racks to cool completely.

Nutritional Information (per cookie):
- Calories: 120
- Carbohydrates: 19g
- Protein: 2g
- Fat: 4g
- Fiber: 1g
- Sugar: 9g

- Sodium: 85mg

Tips:

- Decorate the cookies with royal icing for a festive touch.
- For a softer cookie, bake for the minimum time.
- The dough can be made ahead and refrigerated for up to 3 days or frozen for up to 1 month.

Shortbread Cookies

Prep Time: 15 minutes (plus 30 minutes chilling time)
Cook Time: 20-25 minutes
Servings: 24 cookies
Ingredients:

- 2 cups all-purpose flour
- 1/2 cup granulated sugar
- 1 cup unsalted butter, softened
- 1 tsp vanilla extract
- 1/4 tsp salt

Instructions:

1. **Preheat the Oven:**
   - Preheat your oven to 325°F (165°C). Line two baking sheets with parchment paper.
2. **Mix Dry Ingredients:**
   - In a medium bowl, whisk together the flour and salt.
3. **Cream Butter and Sugar:**
   - In the bowl of your KitchenAid stand mixer, beat the butter and sugar on medium speed until creamy.
4. **Add Vanilla:**
   - Add the vanilla extract and mix until combined.
5. **Combine Wet and Dry Ingredients:**
   - Gradually add the flour mixture to the butter mixture, mixing on low speed until the dough comes together.

6. **Chill the Dough:**
   - Form the dough into a disc, wrap in plastic wrap, and refrigerate for at least 30 minutes.
7. **Shape the Cookies:**
   - Roll out the dough on a lightly floured surface to 1/4-inch thickness.
   - Cut into desired shapes with cookie cutters and place on the prepared baking sheets.
8. **Bake the Cookies:**
   - Bake for 20-25 minutes, or until the edges are lightly golden.
   - Remove from the oven and let the cookies cool on the baking sheets for 5 minutes, then transfer to wire racks to cool completely.

Nutritional Information (per cookie):
- Calories: 110
- Carbohydrates: 13g
- Protein: 1g
- Fat: 6g
- Fiber: 0g
- Sugar: 5g
- Sodium: 30mg

Tips:
- For a classic presentation, prick the tops of the cookies with a fork before baking.
- The dough can be flavored with lemon zest, almond extract, or other flavorings.
- Shortbread cookies can be dipped in melted chocolate for a delicious variation.

Macarons

Prep Time: 30 minutes (plus 1 hour resting time)
Cook Time: 15-18 minutes
Servings: 24 macarons

Ingredients:

- 1 3/4 cups powdered sugar
- 1 cup almond flour
- 3 large egg whites, room temperature
- 1/4 cup granulated sugar
- 1/4 tsp cream of tartar
- Food coloring (optional)
- Filling of your choice (buttercream, ganache, etc.)

Instructions:

1. **Prepare Dry Ingredients:**
   - In a food processor, pulse the powdered sugar and almond flour until finely ground. Sift the mixture through a fine-mesh sieve into a bowl.

2. **Beat Egg Whites:**
   - In the bowl of your KitchenAid stand mixer, beat the egg whites and cream of tartar on medium speed until frothy.
   - Gradually add the granulated sugar, increasing the speed to high, and beat until stiff peaks form.
   - Add food coloring if desired.

3. **Combine Wet and Dry Ingredients:**
   - Gently fold the almond flour mixture into the egg whites until the batter flows like lava. Do not overmix.
4. **Pipe the Macarons:**
   - Transfer the batter to a piping bag fitted with a round tip.
   - Pipe small circles (about 1 inch in diameter) onto a baking sheet lined with parchment paper.
   - Tap the baking sheet firmly on the counter to release any air bubbles.
5. **Rest the Macarons:**
   - Let the macarons sit at room temperature for about 1 hour, or until a skin forms on the surface.
6. **Preheat the Oven:**
   - Preheat your oven to 300°F (150°C).
7. **Bake the Macarons:**
   - Bake for 15-18 minutes, or until the macarons are firm and can be gently lifted from the parchment paper.
   - Let them cool completely on the baking sheet.
8. **Fill the Macarons:**
   - Once cooled, sandwich two macarons together with your chosen filling.

Nutritional Information (per macaron):
- Calories: 90
- Carbohydrates: 14g
- Protein: 2g
- Fat: 3g
- Fiber: 1g
- Sugar: 12g
- Sodium: 10mg

Tips:
- Ensure all utensils are clean and grease-free for the best meringue.
- Aging egg whites (leaving them out at room temperature for 24-48 hours) can improve the texture.
- Store macarons in the refrigerator for up to 5 days or freeze for up to 1 month.

Biscotti

Prep Time: 20 minutes
Cook Time: 35-40 minutes (plus 10-15 minutes second bake)
Servings: 24 biscotti

Ingredients:
- 2 cups all-purpose flour
- 1 cup granulated sugar
- 1 tsp baking powder
- 1/4 tsp salt
- 3 large eggs
- 1 tsp vanilla extract
- 1 cup almonds, toasted and chopped
- 1 tsp almond extract (optional)

Instructions:
1. **Preheat the Oven:**
   - Preheat your oven to 350°F (175°C). Line a baking sheet with parchment paper.
2. **Mix Dry Ingredients:**
   - In a medium bowl, whisk together the flour, sugar, baking powder, and salt.
3. **Combine Wet Ingredients:**
   - In the bowl of your KitchenAid stand mixer, beat the eggs, vanilla extract, and almond extract (if using) on medium speed until combined.

4. **Combine Wet and Dry Ingredients:**
   - Gradually add the flour mixture to the egg mixture, mixing on low speed until combined.
   - Stir in the chopped almonds.
5. **Shape the Dough:**
   - Divide the dough in half and shape each half into a log about 12 inches long and 2 inches wide.
   - Place the logs on the prepared baking sheet.
6. **First Bake:**
   - Bake for 25-30 minutes, or until the logs are golden brown and set.
   - Remove from the oven and let cool for 10 minutes.
7. **Slice the Biscotti:**
   - Reduce the oven temperature to 325°F (165°C).
   - Using a serrated knife, slice the logs diagonally into 1/2-inch thick slices.
   - Place the slices cut side down on the baking sheet.
8. **Second Bake:**
   - Bake for an additional 10-15 minutes, or until the biscotti are crisp and golden.
9. **Cool the Biscotti:**
   - Remove from the oven and let cool completely on wire racks.

Nutritional Information (per biscotti):

- Calories: 110
- Carbohydrates: 18g
- Protein: 3g
- Fat: 3g
- Fiber: 1g
- Sugar: 9g
- Sodium: 60mg

Tips:

- Biscotti can be dipped in melted chocolate for added flavor.
- Store biscotti in an airtight container to maintain their crisp texture.
- Experiment with different nuts and dried fruits for varied flavors.

CAKES

Classic Vanilla Cake

Prep Time: 20 minutes
Cook Time: 25-30 minutes
Servings: 12 slices
Ingredients:
- 2 1/2 cups all-purpose flour
- 2 1/2 tsp baking powder
- 1/2 tsp salt
- 1 1/2 cups granulated sugar
- 3/4 cup unsalted butter, softened
- 4 large eggs
- 1 tbsp vanilla extract
- 1 cup whole milk

Instructions:
1. **Preheat the Oven:**
   - Preheat your oven to 350°F (175°C). Grease and flour two 9-inch round cake pans.
2. **Mix Dry Ingredients:**
   - In a medium bowl, whisk together the flour, baking powder, and salt.
3. **Cream Butter and Sugar:**
   - In the bowl of your KitchenAid stand mixer, beat the butter and sugar on medium speed until light and fluffy.
4. **Add Eggs and Vanilla:**

- Add the eggs one at a time, beating well after each addition. Stir in the vanilla extract.

5. **Combine Wet and Dry Ingredients:**
   - Gradually add the flour mixture to the butter mixture alternately with the milk, beginning and ending with the flour mixture. Mix until just combined.

6. **Bake the Cake:**
   - Divide the batter evenly between the prepared pans and smooth the tops.
   - Bake for 25-30 minutes, or until a toothpick inserted into the center comes out clean.
   - Remove from the oven and let the cakes cool in the pans for 10 minutes, then transfer to wire racks to cool completely.

Nutritional Information (per slice):
- Calories: 310
- Carbohydrates: 42g
- Protein: 4g
- Fat: 15g
- Fiber: 1g
- Sugar: 27g
- Sodium: 200mg

Tips:
- Ensure the butter is at room temperature for easy creaming.
- For added flavor, use vanilla bean paste instead of vanilla extract.
- Pair this cake with your favorite frosting, such as buttercream or cream cheese frosting.

Chocolate Fudge Cake

Prep Time: 25 minutes
Cook Time: 30-35 minutes
Servings: 12 slices
Ingredients:
- 1 3/4 cups all-purpose flour
- 1 1/2 tsp baking powder
- 1 1/2 tsp baking soda
- 1 cup unsweetened cocoa powder
- 2 cups granulated sugar
- 1/2 tsp salt
- 1 cup buttermilk
- 1/2 cup vegetable oil
- 2 large eggs
- 2 tsp vanilla extract
- 1 cup boiling water

Instructions:
1. **Preheat the Oven:**
   - Preheat your oven to 350°F (175°C). Grease and flour two 9-inch round cake pans.
2. **Mix Dry Ingredients:**
   - In a large bowl, whisk together the flour, baking powder, baking soda, cocoa powder, sugar, and salt.
3. **Combine Wet Ingredients:**
   - In the bowl of your KitchenAid stand mixer, combine the buttermilk, vegetable oil, eggs, and vanilla extract. Beat on medium speed until well combined.

4. **Combine Wet and Dry Ingredients:**
   - Gradually add the dry ingredients to the wet ingredients, mixing on low speed until combined.
   - Slowly add the boiling water, mixing until the batter is smooth.
5. **Bake the Cake:**
   - Divide the batter evenly between the prepared pans and smooth the tops.
   - Bake for 30-35 minutes, or until a toothpick inserted into the center comes out clean.
   - Remove from the oven and let the cakes cool in the pans for 10 minutes, then transfer to wire racks to cool completely.

Nutritional Information (per slice):
- Calories: 360
- Carbohydrates: 58g
- Protein: 4g
- Fat: 15g
- Fiber: 3g
- Sugar: 38g
- Sodium: 250mg

Tips:
- For a richer flavor, use Dutch-processed cocoa powder.
- Add a layer of chocolate ganache or fudge frosting between the cake layers for an extra indulgent treat.
- Ensure all ingredients are at room temperature for the best results.

Red Velvet Cake

Prep Time: 25 minutes
Cook Time: 30-35 minutes
Servings: 12 slices
Ingredients:

- 2 1/2 cups all-purpose flour
- 2 tbsp unsweetened cocoa powder
- 1 1/2 tsp baking soda
- 1/2 tsp salt
- 1 1/2 cups granulated sugar
- 1 cup vegetable oil
- 2 large eggs
- 1 tsp vanilla extract
- 1 tsp white vinegar
- 1 cup buttermilk
- 2 tbsp red food coloring

Instructions:

1. **Preheat the Oven:**
   - Preheat your oven to 350°F (175°C). Grease and flour two 9-inch round cake pans.
2. **Mix Dry Ingredients:**
   - In a medium bowl, whisk together the flour, cocoa powder, baking soda, and salt.
3. **Combine Wet Ingredients:**
   - In the bowl of your KitchenAid stand mixer, beat the sugar and oil on medium speed until well combined.
   - Add the eggs, one at a time, beating well after each addition. Stir in the vanilla extract and white vinegar.

4. **Combine Wet and Dry Ingredients:**
    o Gradually add the flour mixture to the wet ingredients alternately with the buttermilk, beginning and ending with the flour mixture. Mix until just combined.
    o Add the red food coloring and mix until the batter is evenly colored.
5. **Bake the Cake:**
    o Divide the batter evenly between the prepared pans and smooth the tops.
    o Bake for 30-35 minutes, or until a toothpick inserted into the center comes out clean.
    o Remove from the oven and let the cakes cool in the pans for 10 minutes, then transfer to wire racks to cool completely.

Nutritional Information (per slice):
- Calories: 350
- Carbohydrates: 45g
- Protein: 4g
- Fat: 18g
- Fiber: 1g
- Sugar: 30g
- Sodium: 300mg

Tips:
- For a deeper red color, use gel food coloring instead of liquid.
- Pair this cake with a classic cream cheese frosting for a delicious combination.
- Ensure the layers are completely cool before frosting to prevent the frosting from melting.

Carrot Cake

Prep Time: 20 minutes
Cook Time: 35-40 minutes
Servings: 12 slices
Ingredients:
- 2 cups all-purpose flour
- 2 tsp baking powder
- 1 1/2 tsp baking soda
- 1 1/2 tsp ground cinnamon
- 1/2 tsp ground nutmeg
- 1/2 tsp ground ginger
- 1/2 tsp salt
- 1 cup granulated sugar
- 1 cup packed brown sugar
- 1 cup vegetable oil
- 4 large eggs
- 1 tsp vanilla extract
- 3 cups grated carrots
- 1 cup crushed pineapple, drained
- 1/2 cup chopped walnuts (optional)
- 1/2 cup raisins (optional)

Instructions:
1. **Preheat the Oven:**
   - Preheat your oven to 350°F (175°C). Grease and flour two 9-inch round cake pans.
2. **Mix Dry Ingredients:**

o   In a medium bowl, whisk together the flour, baking powder, baking soda, cinnamon, nutmeg, ginger, and salt.

3. **Combine Wet Ingredients:**
   o   In the bowl of your KitchenAid stand mixer, beat the granulated sugar, brown sugar, and oil on medium speed until well combined.
   o   Add the eggs one at a time, beating well after each addition. Stir in the vanilla extract.

4. **Combine Wet and Dry Ingredients:**
   o   Gradually add the flour mixture to the wet ingredients, mixing on low speed until combined.
   o   Fold in the grated carrots, crushed pineapple, walnuts, and raisins.

5. **Bake the Cake:**
   o   Divide the batter evenly between the prepared pans and smooth the tops.
   o   Bake for 35-40 minutes, or until a toothpick inserted into the center comes out clean.
   o   Remove from the oven and let the cakes cool in the pans for 10 minutes, then transfer to wire racks to cool completely.

Nutritional Information (per slice):
- Calories: 400
- Carbohydrates: 55g
- Protein: 5g
- Fat: 18g

- Fiber: 2g
- Sugar: 35g
- Sodium: 300mg

Tips:

- For extra moistness, use freshly grated carrots.
- Pair the cake with a classic cream cheese frosting for the best flavor.
- Add a hint of orange zest to the frosting for a citrusy twist.

Lemon Drizzle Cake

Prep Time: 15 minutes
Cook Time: 45-50 minutes
Servings: 12 slices

Ingredients:

- 1 1/2 cups all-purpose flour
- 1 tsp baking powder
- 1/2 tsp salt
- 1 cup unsalted butter, softened
- 1 cup granulated sugar
- 4 large eggs
- 2 tbsp lemon zest
- 1/4 cup fresh lemon juice
- 1/2 cup whole milk

For the Lemon Syrup:

- 1/2 cup granulated sugar
- 1/2 cup fresh lemon juice

Instructions:

1. **Preheat the Oven:**
   - Preheat your oven to 350°F (175°C). Grease and flour a 9x5-inch loaf pan.
2. **Mix Dry Ingredients:**
   - In a medium bowl, whisk together the flour, baking powder, and salt.
3. **Cream Butter and Sugar:**
   - In the bowl of your KitchenAid stand mixer, beat the butter and sugar on medium speed until light and fluffy.

4. **Add Eggs and Lemon Zest:**
   - Add the eggs one at a time, beating well after each addition. Stir in the lemon zest and lemon juice.
5. **Combine Wet and Dry Ingredients:**
   - Gradually add the flour mixture to the butter mixture alternately with the milk, beginning and ending with the flour mixture. Mix until just combined.
6. **Bake the Cake:**
   - Pour the batter into the prepared loaf pan and smooth the top.
   - Bake for 45-50 minutes, or until a toothpick inserted into the center comes out clean.
   - Remove from the oven and let the cake cool in the pan for 10 minutes, then transfer to a wire rack.
7. **Make the Lemon Syrup:**
   - In a small saucepan, combine the sugar and lemon juice. Heat over medium heat until the sugar dissolves.
8. **Drizzle the Cake:**
   - While the cake is still warm, poke holes in the top with a skewer and pour the lemon syrup over the cake.
   - Let the cake cool completely before slicing.

Nutritional Information (per slice):
- Calories: 300
- Carbohydrates: 40g

- Protein: 4g
- Fat: 14g
- Fiber: 1g
- Sugar: 30g
- Sodium: 150mg

Tips:

- For a more intense lemon flavor, add a bit of lemon extract to the batter.
- The cake can be topped with a simple lemon glaze made from powdered sugar and lemon juice.
- Store the cake in an airtight container to keep it moist.

Angel Food Cake

Prep Time: 20 minutes
Cook Time: 35-40 minutes
Servings: 12 slices
Ingredients:
- 1 cup cake flour
- 1 1/2 cups granulated sugar, divided
- 12 large egg whites, room temperature
- 1 tsp cream of tartar
- 1/4 tsp salt
- 1 tsp vanilla extract
- 1/2 tsp almond extract (optional)

Instructions:
1. **Preheat the Oven:**
   - Preheat your oven to 350°F (175°C). Have an ungreased 10-inch tube pan ready.
2. **Prepare Dry Ingredients:**
   - Sift the cake flour and 3/4 cup of granulated sugar together. Set aside.
3. **Beat Egg Whites:**
   - In the bowl of your KitchenAid stand mixer, beat the egg whites, cream of tartar, and salt on medium speed until foamy.
   - Gradually add the remaining 3/4 cup of granulated sugar, one tablespoon at a time, beating on high speed until stiff, glossy peaks form.
   - Stir in the vanilla extract and almond extract (if using).

4. **Fold in Dry Ingredients:**
    o   Gradually fold the flour mixture into the egg whites, about 1/4 cup at a time, using a spatula. Be gentle to avoid deflating the batter.
5. **Bake the Cake:**
    o   Pour the batter into the ungreased tube pan and smooth the top.
    o   Bake for 35-40 minutes, or until a toothpick inserted into the center comes out clean.
    o   Remove from the oven and invert the pan to cool completely.
6. **Remove from the Pan:**
    o   Once the cake is completely cool, run a knife around the edges to loosen it from the pan and remove the cake.

Nutritional Information (per slice):
*   Calories: 120
*   Carbohydrates: 26g
*   Protein: 3g
*   Fat: 0g
*   Fiber: 0g
*   Sugar: 22g
*   Sodium: 150mg

Tips:
*   Ensure the egg whites are at room temperature for the best volume.
*   Use a serrated knife to gently cut the cake to avoid squishing it.
*   Pair with fresh berries and whipped cream for a delightful dessert.

Pound Cake

Prep Time: 20 minutes
Cook Time: 1 hour 15 minutes
Servings: 12 slices

Ingredients:

- 2 cups all-purpose flour
- 1 tsp baking powder
- 1/2 tsp salt
- 1 cup unsalted butter, softened
- 1 1/2 cups granulated sugar
- 4 large eggs
- 1 tsp vanilla extract
- 1/2 cup whole milk

Instructions:

1. **Preheat the Oven:**
   - Preheat your oven to 350°F (175°C). Grease and flour a 9x5-inch loaf pan.
2. **Mix Dry Ingredients:**
   - In a medium bowl, whisk together the flour, baking powder, and salt.
3. **Cream Butter and Sugar:**
   - In the bowl of your KitchenAid stand mixer, beat the butter and sugar on medium speed until light and fluffy.
4. **Add Eggs and Vanilla:**
   - Add the eggs one at a time, beating well after each addition. Stir in the vanilla extract.

5. **Combine Wet and Dry Ingredients:**
   - o Gradually add the flour mixture to the butter mixture alternately with the milk, beginning and ending with the flour mixture. Mix until just combined.
6. **Bake the Cake:**
   - o Pour the batter into the prepared loaf pan and smooth the top.
   - o Bake for 1 hour 15 minutes, or until a toothpick inserted into the center comes out clean.
   - o Remove from the oven and let the cake cool in the pan for 10 minutes, then transfer to a wire rack to cool completely.

Nutritional Information (per slice):
- Calories: 320
- Carbohydrates: 42g
- Protein: 5g
- Fat: 15g
- Fiber: 1g
- Sugar: 28g
- Sodium: 200mg

Tips:
- For a richer flavor, add a teaspoon of almond extract along with the vanilla.
- Serve with fresh berries and whipped cream for an extra touch.
- Ensure all ingredients are at room temperature for the best results.

Bundt Cake

Prep Time: 20 minutes
Cook Time: 50-60 minutes
Servings: 12 slices
Ingredients:
- 3 cups all-purpose flour
- 2 tsp baking powder
- 1/2 tsp baking soda
- 1/2 tsp salt
- 1 cup unsalted butter, softened
- 2 cups granulated sugar
- 4 large eggs
- 1 tsp vanilla extract
- 1 cup sour cream
- 1/2 cup whole milk

Instructions:
1. **Preheat the Oven:**
   - Preheat your oven to 350°F (175°C). Grease and flour a Bundt pan.
2. **Mix Dry Ingredients:**
   - In a medium bowl, whisk together the flour, baking powder, baking soda, and salt.
3. **Cream Butter and Sugar:**
   - In the bowl of your KitchenAid stand mixer, beat the butter and sugar on medium speed until light and fluffy.
4. **Add Eggs and Vanilla:**
   - Add the eggs one at a time, beating well after each addition. Stir in the vanilla extract.

5. **Combine Wet and Dry Ingredients:**
   o Gradually add the flour mixture to the butter mixture alternately with the sour cream and milk, beginning and ending with the flour mixture. Mix until just combined.
6. **Bake the Cake:**
   o Pour the batter into the prepared Bundt pan and smooth the top.
   o Bake for 50-60 minutes, or until a toothpick inserted into the center comes out clean.
   o Remove from the oven and let the cake cool in the pan for 10 minutes, then transfer to a wire rack to cool completely.

Nutritional Information (per slice):
- Calories: 380
- Carbohydrates: 50g
- Protein: 6g
- Fat: 18g
- Fiber: 1g
- Sugar: 30g
- Sodium: 250mg

Tips:
- Dust the cooled cake with powdered sugar or drizzle with a glaze for a beautiful presentation.
- Add lemon or orange zest to the batter for a citrusy twist.
- Ensure the Bundt pan is well-greased to prevent sticking.

Cheesecake

Prep Time: 20 minutes (plus chilling time)
Cook Time: 1 hour
Servings: 12 slices
Ingredients:
For the Crust:
- 1 1/2 cups graham cracker crumbs
- 1/4 cup granulated sugar
- 1/2 cup unsalted butter, melted

For the Filling:
- 4 packages (8 oz each) cream cheese, softened
- 1 cup granulated sugar
- 1 tsp vanilla extract
- 4 large eggs
- 1 cup sour cream

Instructions:
1. **Preheat the Oven:**
   o Preheat your oven to 325°F (165°C). Grease a 9-inch springform pan.
2. **Make the Crust:**
   o In a medium bowl, combine the graham cracker crumbs, sugar, and melted butter. Press the mixture into the bottom of the prepared pan.
3. **Mix the Filling:**
   o In the bowl of your KitchenAid stand mixer, beat the cream cheese and sugar on medium speed until smooth.

- o Add the vanilla extract and eggs, one at a time, beating well after each addition.
- o Stir in the sour cream until well combined.

4. **Bake the Cheesecake:**
   - o Pour the filling over the crust in the pan.
   - o Bake for 55-60 minutes, or until the center is set and the edges are lightly browned.
   - o Turn off the oven and let the cheesecake cool in the oven with the door slightly ajar for 1 hour.
   - o Remove from the oven and refrigerate for at least 4 hours or overnight.

5. **Serve:**
   - o Remove the cheesecake from the springform pan and slice to serve.

Nutritional Information (per slice):
- Calories: 450
- Carbohydrates: 33g
- Protein: 8g
- Fat: 33g
- Fiber: 0g
- Sugar: 27g
- Sodium: 350mg

Tips:
- For a perfect texture, ensure all ingredients are at room temperature before mixing.
- Serve with fresh berries, fruit compote, or chocolate sauce for added flavor.
- Use a water bath to prevent cracks in the cheesecake.

Tiramisu Cake

Prep Time: 30 minutes (plus chilling time)
Cook Time: 25-30 minutes
Servings: 12 slices
Ingredients:
For the Cake:

- 1 1/2 cups all-purpose flour
- 1 tsp baking powder
- 1/2 tsp baking soda
- 1/4 tsp salt
- 1/2 cup unsalted butter, softened
- 1 cup granulated sugar
- 2 large eggs
- 1 tsp vanilla extract
- 1 cup whole milk

For the Filling:

- 1 cup strong brewed coffee, cooled
- 2 tbsp coffee liqueur (optional)
- 1/4 cup granulated sugar
- 8 oz mascarpone cheese
- 1 cup heavy cream
- 1/4 cup powdered sugar
- 1 tsp vanilla extract
- Unsweetened cocoa powder for dusting

Instructions:

1. **Preheat the Oven:**
   - Preheat your oven to 350°F (175°C). Grease and flour two 9-inch round cake pans.
2. **Mix Dry Ingredients:**
   - In a medium bowl, whisk together the flour, baking powder, baking soda, and salt.

3. **Cream Butter and Sugar:**
   - In the bowl of your KitchenAid stand mixer, beat the butter and sugar on medium speed until light and fluffy.
4. **Add Eggs and Vanilla:**
   - Add the eggs one at a time, beating well after each addition. Stir in the vanilla extract.
5. **Combine Wet and Dry Ingredients:**
   - Gradually add the flour mixture to the butter mixture alternately with the milk, beginning and ending with the flour mixture. Mix until just combined.
6. **Bake the Cake:**
   - Divide the batter evenly between the prepared pans and smooth the tops.
   - Bake for 25-30 minutes, or until a toothpick inserted into the center comes out clean.
   - Remove from the oven and let the cakes cool in the pans for 10 minutes, then transfer to wire racks to cool completely.
7. **Make the Filling:**
   - In a small bowl, combine the coffee and coffee liqueur (if using). Set aside.
   - In the bowl of your KitchenAid stand mixer, beat the mascarpone cheese, heavy cream, powdered sugar, and vanilla extract on medium speed until stiff peaks form.

8. **Assemble the Cake:**
   - Place one cake layer on a serving plate. Brush generously with the coffee mixture.
   - Spread half of the mascarpone filling over the cake layer.
   - Place the second cake layer on top and brush with the remaining coffee mixture.
   - Spread the remaining mascarpone filling over the top and sides of the cake.
9. **Chill the Cake:**
   - Refrigerate the cake for at least 2 hours or overnight to allow the flavors to meld.
10. **Serve:** Before serving, dust the top of the cake with unsweetened cocoa powder.

Nutritional Information (per slice):
- Calories: 420
- Carbohydrates: 44g
- Protein: 6g
- Fat: 26g
- Fiber: 1g
- Sugar: 28g
- Sodium: 200mg

Tips:
- Ensure the coffee is completely cooled before brushing on the cake to prevent it from becoming soggy.
- For an extra coffee kick, add a teaspoon of instant coffee granules to the filling.
- Garnish with chocolate shavings or chocolate curls for a decorative touch.

ICE CREAM

Vanilla Bean Ice Cream

Prep Time: 30 minutes (plus chilling and freezing time)
Cook Time: 10 minutes
Servings: 1 quart

Ingredients:

- 2 cups heavy cream
- 1 cup whole milk
- 3/4 cup granulated sugar
- 1 vanilla bean
- 5 large egg yolks
- 1 tsp vanilla extract

Instructions:

1. **Prepare the Vanilla Bean:**
   - Split the vanilla bean lengthwise and scrape out the seeds.
2. **Heat the Cream Mixture:**
   - In a medium saucepan, combine the heavy cream, milk, half of the sugar, vanilla bean seeds, and the vanilla bean pod. Heat over medium heat until it begins to steam, but do not boil.
3. **Whisk the Egg Yolks:**
   - In a medium bowl, whisk the egg yolks with the remaining sugar until pale and thick.

4. **Temper the Egg Yolks:**
   - Gradually pour about 1/2 cup of the hot cream mixture into the egg yolks, whisking constantly to temper the yolks.
   - Pour the tempered yolk mixture back into the saucepan with the remaining cream mixture.
5. **Cook the Custard:**
   - Cook over medium heat, stirring constantly with a wooden spoon, until the mixture thickens and coats the back of the spoon, about 5-7 minutes. Do not let it boil.
6. **Strain and Chill:**
   - Strain the custard through a fine-mesh sieve into a clean bowl. Stir in the vanilla extract.
   - Cover the bowl with plastic wrap, pressing it directly onto the surface of the custard to prevent a skin from forming. Chill in the refrigerator for at least 4 hours or overnight.
7. **Churn the Ice Cream:**
   - Pour the chilled custard into your KitchenAid ice cream maker attachment and churn according to the manufacturer's instructions.
8. **Freeze the Ice Cream:**
   - Transfer the churned ice cream to an airtight container and freeze for at least 4 hours before serving.

Nutritional Information (per 1/2 cup serving):

- Calories: 250
- Carbohydrates: 20g
- Protein: 4g
- Fat: 18g
- Fiber: 0g
- Sugar: 19g
- Sodium: 50mg

Tips:

- For an extra vanilla flavor, add a splash of vanilla extract after churning.
- Use the highest quality vanilla bean for the best flavor.
- Serve with fresh berries or your favorite dessert toppings.

Chocolate Ice Cream

Prep Time: 30 minutes (plus chilling and freezing time)
Cook Time: 10 minutes
Servings: 1 quart

Ingredients:

- 2 cups heavy cream
- 1 cup whole milk
- 3/4 cup granulated sugar
- 1/2 cup unsweetened cocoa powder
- 4 large egg yolks
- 1 tsp vanilla extract
- 4 oz semi-sweet chocolate, finely chopped

Instructions:

1. **Heat the Cream Mixture:**
   o In a medium saucepan, combine the heavy cream, milk, sugar, and cocoa powder. Heat over medium heat until it begins to steam, but do not boil. Whisk to dissolve the cocoa powder.

2. **Whisk the Egg Yolks:**
   o In a medium bowl, whisk the egg yolks until pale and thick.

3. **Temper the Egg Yolks:**
   o Gradually pour about 1/2 cup of the hot cream mixture into the egg yolks, whisking constantly to temper the yolks.

- o Pour the tempered yolk mixture back into the saucepan with the remaining cream mixture.
4. **Cook the Custard:**
   - o Cook over medium heat, stirring constantly with a wooden spoon, until the mixture thickens and coats the back of the spoon, about 5-7 minutes. Do not let it boil.
5. **Add the Chocolate:**
   - o Remove the saucepan from the heat and stir in the chopped chocolate until melted and smooth.
6. **Strain and Chill:**
   - o Strain the custard through a fine-mesh sieve into a clean bowl. Stir in the vanilla extract.
   - o Cover the bowl with plastic wrap, pressing it directly onto the surface of the custard to prevent a skin from forming. Chill in the refrigerator for at least 4 hours or overnight.
7. **Churn the Ice Cream:**
   - o Pour the chilled custard into your KitchenAid ice cream maker attachment and churn according to the manufacturer's instructions.
8. **Freeze the Ice Cream:**
   - o Transfer the churned ice cream to an airtight container and freeze for at least 4 hours before serving.

Nutritional Information (per 1/2 cup serving):

- Calories: 280
- Carbohydrates: 23g
- Protein: 5g
- Fat: 19g
- Fiber: 2g
- Sugar: 21g
- Sodium: 60mg

Tips:

- For a richer chocolate flavor, use dark chocolate instead of semi-sweet.
- Add chocolate chips or chunks during the last few minutes of churning for extra texture.
- Serve with a drizzle of chocolate sauce or a sprinkle of cocoa powder.

Strawberry Ice Cream

Prep Time: 30 minutes (plus chilling and freezing time)
Cook Time: 10 minutes
Servings: 1 quart

Ingredients:

- 2 cups heavy cream
- 1 cup whole milk
- 3/4 cup granulated sugar
- 1 vanilla bean
- 5 large egg yolks
- 1 tsp vanilla extract
- 1 pound fresh strawberries, hulled and chopped
- 1/4 cup granulated sugar (for strawberries)

Instructions:

1. **Prepare the Vanilla Bean:**
   - Split the vanilla bean lengthwise and scrape out the seeds.
2. **Heat the Cream Mixture:**
   - In a medium saucepan, combine the heavy cream, milk, half of the sugar, vanilla bean seeds, and the vanilla bean pod. Heat over medium heat until it begins to steam, but do not boil.
3. **Whisk the Egg Yolks:**
   - In a medium bowl, whisk the egg yolks with the remaining sugar until pale and thick.
4. **Temper the Egg Yolks:**

o Gradually pour about 1/2 cup of the hot
  cream mixture into the egg yolks, whisking
  constantly to temper the yolks.
o Pour the tempered yolk mixture back into
  the saucepan with the remaining cream
  mixture.

5. **Cook the Custard:**
   o Cook over medium heat, stirring constantly
     with a wooden spoon, until the mixture
     thickens and coats the back of the spoon,
     about 5-7 minutes. Do not let it boil.

6. **Strain and Chill:**
   o Strain the custard through a fine-mesh sieve
     into a clean bowl. Stir in the vanilla extract.
   o Cover the bowl with plastic wrap, pressing it
     directly onto the surface of the custard to
     prevent a skin from forming. Chill in the
     refrigerator for at least 4 hours or overnight.

7. **Prepare the Strawberries:**
   o In a small saucepan, combine the chopped
     strawberries and 1/4 cup of sugar. Cook over
     medium heat until the strawberries are soft
     and the sugar has dissolved. Let cool, then
     puree in a blender until smooth.

8. **Combine and Churn:**
   o Stir the strawberry puree into the chilled
     custard.

- Pour the mixture into your KitchenAid ice cream maker attachment and churn according to the manufacturer's instructions.
9. **Freeze the Ice Cream:**
   - Transfer the churned ice cream to an airtight container and freeze for at least 4 hours before serving.

Nutritional Information (per 1/2 cup serving):
- Calories: 260
- Carbohydrates: 26g
- Protein: 4g
- Fat: 17g
- Fiber: 1g
- Sugar: 24g
- Sodium: 50mg

Tips:
- For chunks of strawberries in your ice cream, reserve some of the cooked strawberries and stir them into the ice cream after churning.
- Use fresh, ripe strawberries for the best flavor.
- Serve with fresh strawberry slices or a dollop of whipped cream.

Mint Chocolate Chip Ice Cream

Prep Time: 30 minutes (plus chilling and freezing time)
Cook Time: 10 minutes
Servings: 1 quart

Ingredients:

- 2 cups heavy cream
- 1 cup whole milk
- 3/4 cup granulated sugar
- 1 tsp peppermint extract
- 5 large egg yolks
- 1 tsp vanilla extract
- Green food coloring (optional)
- 1 cup mini chocolate chips or chopped chocolate

Instructions:

1. **Heat the Cream Mixture:**
   - In a medium saucepan, combine the heavy cream, milk, and half of the sugar. Heat over medium heat until it begins to steam, but do not boil.
2. **Whisk the Egg Yolks:**
   - In a medium bowl, whisk the egg yolks with the remaining sugar until pale and thick.
3. **Temper the Egg Yolks:**
   - Gradually pour about 1/2 cup of the hot cream mixture into the egg yolks, whisking constantly to temper the yolks.

- Pour the tempered yolk mixture back into the saucepan with the remaining cream mixture.

4. **Cook the Custard:**
   - Cook over medium heat, stirring constantly with a wooden spoon, until the mixture thickens and coats the back of the spoon, about 5-7 minutes. Do not let it boil.

5. **Add Peppermint and Vanilla Extracts:**
   - Remove the saucepan from the heat and stir in the peppermint extract and vanilla extract. Add green food coloring if desired.

6. **Strain and Chill:**
   - Strain the custard through a fine-mesh sieve into a clean bowl.
   - Cover the bowl with plastic wrap, pressing it directly onto the surface of the custard to prevent a skin from forming. Chill in the refrigerator for at least 4 hours or overnight.

7. **Churn the Ice Cream:**
   - Pour the chilled custard into your KitchenAid ice cream maker attachment and churn according to the manufacturer's instructions.

8. **Add Chocolate Chips:**
   - During the last few minutes of churning, add the mini chocolate chips or chopped chocolate.

9. **Freeze the Ice Cream:**

- Transfer the churned ice cream to an airtight container and freeze for at least 4 hours before serving.

Nutritional Information (per 1/2 cup serving):

- Calories: 270
- Carbohydrates: 25g
- Protein: 4g
- Fat: 18g
- Fiber: 1g
- Sugar: 23g
- Sodium: 50mg

Tips:

- For a stronger mint flavor, add more peppermint extract, but be careful as it can be overpowering.
- Use dark chocolate chips for a richer flavor.
- Serve with a sprig of fresh mint or chocolate shavings for garnish.

Cookies and Cream Ice Cream

Prep Time: 30 minutes (plus chilling and freezing time)
Cook Time: 10 minutes
Servings: 1 quart

Ingredients:

- 2 cups heavy cream
- 1 cup whole milk
- 3/4 cup granulated sugar
- 1 vanilla bean
- 5 large egg yolks
- 1 tsp vanilla extract
- 15 chocolate sandwich cookies (such as Oreos), roughly chopped

Instructions:

1. **Prepare the Vanilla Bean:**
   - Split the vanilla bean lengthwise and scrape out the seeds.
2. **Heat the Cream Mixture:**
   - In a medium saucepan, combine the heavy cream, milk, half of the sugar, vanilla bean seeds, and the vanilla bean pod. Heat over medium heat until it begins to steam, but do not boil.
3. **Whisk the Egg Yolks:**
   - In a medium bowl, whisk the egg yolks with the remaining sugar until pale and thick.
4. **Temper the Egg Yolks:**

- Gradually pour about 1/2 cup of the hot cream mixture into the egg yolks, whisking constantly to temper the yolks.
- Pour the tempered yolk mixture back into the saucepan with the remaining cream mixture.

5. **Cook the Custard:**
   - Cook over medium heat, stirring constantly with a wooden spoon, until the mixture thickens and coats the back of the spoon, about 5-7 minutes. Do not let it boil.

6. **Strain and Chill:**
   - Strain the custard through a fine-mesh sieve into a clean bowl. Stir in the vanilla extract.
   - Cover the bowl with plastic wrap, pressing it directly onto the surface of the custard to prevent a skin from forming. Chill in the refrigerator for at least 4 hours or overnight.

7. **Churn the Ice Cream:**
   - Pour the chilled custard into your KitchenAid ice cream maker attachment and churn according to the manufacturer's instructions.

8. **Add Cookies:**
   - During the last few minutes of churning, add the chopped chocolate sandwich cookies.

9. **Freeze the Ice Cream:**

- Transfer the churned ice cream to an airtight container and freeze for at least 4 hours before serving.

Nutritional Information (per 1/2 cup serving):
- Calories: 290
- Carbohydrates: 29g
- Protein: 4g
- Fat: 18g
- Fiber: 1g
- Sugar: 23g
- Sodium: 120mg

Tips:
- Use high-quality chocolate sandwich cookies for the best flavor.
- For a twist, use flavored sandwich cookies like mint or peanut butter.
- Serve with additional crushed cookies on top.

Pistachio Ice Cream

Prep Time: 30 minutes (plus chilling and freezing time)
Cook Time: 10 minutes
Servings: 1 quart
Ingredients:

- 2 cups heavy cream
- 1 cup whole milk
- 3/4 cup granulated sugar
- 1 cup shelled pistachios
- 5 large egg yolks
- 1 tsp vanilla extract
- Green food coloring (optional)

Instructions:

1. **Heat the Cream Mixture:**
   o In a medium saucepan, combine the heavy cream, milk, and half of the sugar. Heat over medium heat until it begins to steam, but do not boil.
2. **Blend the Pistachios:**
   o In a food processor, grind the pistachios until they are finely ground but not a paste.
3. **Whisk the Egg Yolks:**
   o In a medium bowl, whisk the egg yolks with the remaining sugar until pale and thick.
4. **Temper the Egg Yolks:**
   o Gradually pour about 1/2 cup of the hot cream mixture into the egg yolks, whisking constantly to temper the yolks.

- Pour the tempered yolk mixture back into the saucepan with the remaining cream mixture.

5. **Cook the Custard:**
   - Cook over medium heat, stirring constantly with a wooden spoon, until the mixture thickens and coats the back of the spoon, about 5-7 minutes. Do not let it boil.

6. **Add the Pistachios:**
   - Stir in the ground pistachios and cook for an additional 2 minutes.

7. **Strain and Chill:**
   - Strain the custard through a fine-mesh sieve into a clean bowl to remove any large pistachio pieces. Stir in the vanilla extract and green food coloring if desired.
   - Cover the bowl with plastic wrap, pressing it directly onto the surface of the custard to prevent a skin from forming. Chill in the refrigerator for at least 4 hours or overnight.

8. **Churn the Ice Cream:**
   - Pour the chilled custard into your KitchenAid ice cream maker attachment and churn according to the manufacturer's instructions.

9. **Freeze the Ice Cream:**
   - Transfer the churned ice cream to an airtight container and freeze for at least 4 hours before serving.

Nutritional Information (per 1/2 cup serving):
- Calories: 290
- Carbohydrates: 22g
- Protein: 5g
- Fat: 20g
- Fiber: 2g
- Sugar: 20g
- Sodium: 50mg

Tips:
- Use unsalted pistachios for a better balance of flavors.
- For added texture, fold in chopped pistachios during the last few minutes of churning.
- Serve with a sprinkle of chopped pistachios on top.

Coffee Ice Cream

Prep Time: 30 minutes (plus chilling and freezing time)
Cook Time: 10 minutes
Servings: 1 quart
Ingredients:
- 2 cups heavy cream
- 1 cup whole milk
- 3/4 cup granulated sugar
- 2 tbsp instant coffee granules
- 5 large egg yolks
- 1 tsp vanilla extract

Instructions:
1. **Heat the Cream Mixture:**
   - In a medium saucepan, combine the heavy cream, milk, sugar, and instant coffee granules. Heat over medium heat until it begins to steam, but do not boil. Whisk to dissolve the coffee granules.
2. **Whisk the Egg Yolks:**
   - In a medium bowl, whisk the egg yolks until pale and thick.
3. **Temper the Egg Yolks:**
   - Gradually pour about 1/2 cup of the hot cream mixture into the egg yolks, whisking constantly to temper the yolks.
   - Pour the tempered yolk mixture back into the saucepan with the remaining cream mixture.

4. **Cook the Custard:**
   - Cook over medium heat, stirring constantly with a wooden spoon, until the mixture thickens and coats the back of the spoon, about 5-7 minutes. Do not let it boil.
5. **Strain and Chill:**
   - Strain the custard through a fine-mesh sieve into a clean bowl. Stir in the vanilla extract.
   - Cover the bowl with plastic wrap, pressing it directly onto the surface of the custard to prevent a skin from forming. Chill in the refrigerator for at least 4 hours or overnight.
6. **Churn the Ice Cream:**
   - Pour the chilled custard into your KitchenAid ice cream maker attachment and churn according to the manufacturer's instructions.
7. **Freeze the Ice Cream:**
   - Transfer the churned ice cream to an airtight container and freeze for at least 4 hours before serving.

Nutritional Information (per 1/2 cup serving):
- Calories: 250
- Carbohydrates: 20g
- Protein: 4g
- Fat: 18g
- Fiber: 0g
- Sugar: 19g
- Sodium: 50mg

Tips:

- Adjust the amount of coffee granules to your taste preference for a stronger or milder coffee flavor.
- Add chocolate chips or chunks during the last few minutes of churning for a mocha twist.
- Serve with a drizzle of chocolate or caramel sauce for extra indulgence.

Mango Sorbet

Prep Time: 15 minutes (plus freezing time)
Cook Time: 5 minutes
Servings: 1 quart
Ingredients:
- 4 large ripe mangoes, peeled and diced
- 1 cup water
- 1 cup granulated sugar
- 1 tbsp fresh lime juice

Instructions:
1. **Prepare Simple Syrup:**
   - In a small saucepan, combine the water and sugar. Heat over medium heat until the sugar dissolves completely, creating a simple syrup. Let it cool to room temperature.
2. **Blend Mangoes:**
   - In a blender or food processor, puree the diced mangoes until smooth.
3. **Combine Ingredients:**
   - In a large bowl, combine the mango puree, simple syrup, and lime juice. Mix well.
4. **Chill the Mixture:**
   - Cover the bowl and refrigerate the mixture for at least 2 hours or until thoroughly chilled.
5. **Churn the Sorbet:**
   - Pour the chilled mixture into your KitchenAid ice cream maker attachment and

churn according to the manufacturer's instructions.

6. **Freeze the Sorbet:**
   o Transfer the churned sorbet to an airtight container and freeze for at least 4 hours before serving.

Nutritional Information (per 1/2 cup serving):
- Calories: 110
- Carbohydrates: 28g
- Protein: 1g
- Fat: 0g
- Fiber: 2g
- Sugar: 25g
- Sodium: 0mg

Tips:
- For a smoother texture, strain the mango puree before combining it with the simple syrup.
- Adjust the sweetness by adding more or less sugar to taste.
- Garnish with fresh mint leaves or a slice of lime when serving.

'

Raspberry Gelato

Prep Time: 20 minutes (plus chilling and freezing time)
Cook Time: 10 minutes
Servings: 1 quart
Ingredients:
- 2 cups fresh raspberries
- 1 cup whole milk
- 1 cup heavy cream
- 3/4 cup granulated sugar
- 4 large egg yolks
- 1 tsp lemon juice
- 1 tsp vanilla extract

Instructions:
1. **Blend Raspberries:**
   - In a blender or food processor, puree the raspberries until smooth. Strain the puree through a fine-mesh sieve to remove the seeds. Set aside.
2. **Heat the Milk and Cream:**
   - In a medium saucepan, combine the milk, heavy cream, and half of the sugar. Heat over medium heat until it begins to steam, but do not boil.
3. **Whisk the Egg Yolks:**
   - In a medium bowl, whisk the egg yolks with the remaining sugar until pale and thick.
4. **Temper the Egg Yolks:**

- o Gradually pour about 1/2 cup of the hot milk mixture into the egg yolks, whisking constantly to temper the yolks.
- o Pour the tempered yolk mixture back into the saucepan with the remaining milk mixture.

5. **Cook the Custard:**
   - o Cook over medium heat, stirring constantly with a wooden spoon, until the mixture thickens and coats the back of the spoon, about 5-7 minutes. Do not let it boil.

6. **Combine and Chill:**
   - o Remove the saucepan from the heat and stir in the raspberry puree, lemon juice, and vanilla extract.
   - o Cover the bowl with plastic wrap, pressing it directly onto the surface of the custard to prevent a skin from forming. Chill in the refrigerator for at least 4 hours or overnight.

7. **Churn the Gelato:**
   - o Pour the chilled mixture into your KitchenAid ice cream maker attachment and churn according to the manufacturer's instructions.

8. **Freeze the Gelato:**
   - o Transfer the churned gelato to an airtight container and freeze for at least 4 hours before serving.

Nutritional Information (per 1/2 cup serving):
- Calories: 160
- Carbohydrates: 22g
- Protein: 3g
- Fat: 7g
- Fiber: 3g
- Sugar: 20g
- Sodium: 30mg

Tips:
- For a more intense raspberry flavor, add a few extra fresh raspberries to the custard before chilling.
- Serve with fresh raspberries or a drizzle of raspberry sauce.
- Ensure all ingredients are well-chilled before churning to improve the texture.

Coconut Ice Cream

Prep Time: 30 minutes (plus chilling and freezing time)
Cook Time: 10 minutes
Servings: 1 quart

Ingredients:
- 2 cups coconut milk
- 1 cup heavy cream
- 3/4 cup granulated sugar
- 1/2 tsp salt
- 5 large egg yolks
- 1 tsp vanilla extract
- 1/2 cup shredded coconut (optional)

Instructions:
1. **Heat the Coconut Milk and Cream:**
   - In a medium saucepan, combine the coconut milk, heavy cream, sugar, and salt. Heat over medium heat until it begins to steam, but do not boil.
2. **Whisk the Egg Yolks:**
   - In a medium bowl, whisk the egg yolks until pale and thick.
3. **Temper the Egg Yolks:**
   - Gradually pour about 1/2 cup of the hot coconut milk mixture into the egg yolks, whisking constantly to temper the yolks.
   - Pour the tempered yolk mixture back into the saucepan with the remaining coconut milk mixture.

4. **Cook the Custard:**
    - Cook over medium heat, stirring constantly with a wooden spoon, until the mixture thickens and coats the back of the spoon, about 5-7 minutes. Do not let it boil.
5. **Strain and Chill:**
    - Strain the custard through a fine-mesh sieve into a clean bowl. Stir in the vanilla extract.
    - Cover the bowl with plastic wrap, pressing it directly onto the surface of the custard to prevent a skin from forming. Chill in the refrigerator for at least 4 hours or overnight.
6. **Churn the Ice Cream:**
    - Pour the chilled custard into your KitchenAid ice cream maker attachment and churn according to the manufacturer's instructions.
    - If using, add the shredded coconut during the last few minutes of churning.
7. **Freeze the Ice Cream:**
    - Transfer the churned ice cream to an airtight container and freeze for at least 4 hours before serving.

Nutritional Information (per 1/2 cup serving):
- Calories: 260
- Carbohydrates: 20g
- Protein: 4g
- Fat: 18g
- Fiber: 2g

- Sugar: 18g
- Sodium: 60mg

Tips:

- For a more intense coconut flavor, toast the shredded coconut before adding it to the ice cream.
- Serve with a sprinkle of toasted coconut or a drizzle of chocolate sauce.
- Use full-fat coconut milk for the best texture and flavor.

PASTA

Classic Egg Pasta

Prep Time: 20 minutes
Cook Time: 3-5 minutes
Servings: 4 servings

Ingredients:

- 2 cups all-purpose flour
- 3 large eggs
- 1/2 tsp salt
- 1 tbsp olive oil (optional)

Instructions:

1. **Prepare the Dough:**
   - On a clean work surface, mound the flour and make a well in the center. Crack the eggs into the well and add the salt and olive oil (if using).

2. **Mix the Ingredients:**
   - Using a fork, gently beat the eggs, gradually incorporating the flour from the edges of the well until a dough begins to form.

3. **Knead the Dough:**
   - Once the dough comes together, knead it with your hands for about 8-10 minutes, until it becomes smooth and elastic. If the dough is too sticky, add a little more flour; if it's too dry, add a few drops of water.

4. **Rest the Dough:**
   - Wrap the dough in plastic wrap and let it rest at room temperature for at least 30 minutes.
5. **Roll and Cut the Pasta:**
   - Divide the dough into four portions. Using a pasta roller attachment on your KitchenAid stand mixer, roll out each portion of dough to your desired thickness. Start with the widest setting and gradually work down to the thinner settings.
   - Cut the rolled dough into your desired pasta shape (e.g., fettuccine, tagliatelle).
6. **Cook the Pasta:**
   - Bring a large pot of salted water to a boil. Add the fresh pasta and cook for 3-5 minutes, or until al dente. Fresh pasta cooks much faster than dried pasta, so keep an eye on it.
7. **Serve:**
   - Drain the pasta and serve with your favorite sauce.

Nutritional Information (per serving):
- Calories: 250
- Carbohydrates: 42g
- Protein: 9g
- Fat: 4g
- Fiber: 2g
- Sugar: 1g

- Sodium: 150mg

Tips:

- For a richer flavor, use high-quality eggs.
- If you don't have a pasta roller, you can roll out the dough by hand using a rolling pin.
- Fresh pasta can be dried and stored for later use. Lay the cut pasta on a floured surface and let it dry completely before storing in an airtight container.

Spinach Pasta

Prep Time: 30 minutes
Cook Time: 3-5 minutes
Servings: 4 servings
Ingredients:

- 2 cups all-purpose flour
- 3 large eggs
- 1/2 tsp salt
- 1 cup fresh spinach leaves
- 1 tbsp olive oil (optional)

Instructions:

1. **Prepare the Spinach:**
   - Blanch the spinach in boiling water for 1 minute, then transfer it to a bowl of ice water to cool. Drain and squeeze out any excess water. Finely chop the spinach or puree it in a food processor.
2. **Prepare the Dough:**
   - On a clean work surface, mound the flour and make a well in the center. Crack the eggs into the well and add the salt, olive oil (if using), and chopped spinach.
3. **Mix the Ingredients:**
   - Using a fork, gently beat the eggs and spinach, gradually incorporating the flour from the edges of the well until a dough begins to form.

4. **Knead the Dough:**
   o Once the dough comes together, knead it with your hands for about 8-10 minutes, until it becomes smooth and elastic. If the dough is too sticky, add a little more flour; if it's too dry, add a few drops of water.

5. **Rest the Dough:**
   o Wrap the dough in plastic wrap and let it rest at room temperature for at least 30 minutes.

6. **Roll and Cut the Pasta:**
   o Divide the dough into four portions. Using a pasta roller attachment on your KitchenAid stand mixer, roll out each portion of dough to your desired thickness. Start with the widest setting and gradually work down to the thinner settings.
   o Cut the rolled dough into your desired pasta shape (e.g., fettuccine, tagliatelle).

7. **Cook the Pasta:**
   o Bring a large pot of salted water to a boil. Add the fresh pasta and cook for 3-5 minutes, or until al dente.

8. **Serve:**
   o Drain the pasta and serve with your favorite sauce.

Nutritional Information (per serving):
- Calories: 220
- Carbohydrates: 40g

- Protein: 9g
- Fat: 4g
- Fiber: 3g
- Sugar: 1g
- Sodium: 150mg

Tips:

- For a vibrant green color, use fresh spinach and avoid overcooking it.
- Pair spinach pasta with a light sauce like garlic and olive oil or a creamy Alfredo.
- Fresh spinach pasta can be dried and stored for later use.

Whole Wheat Pasta

Prep Time: 20 minutes
Cook Time: 3-5 minutes
Servings: 4 servings

Ingredients:

- 1 1/2 cups whole wheat flour
- 1/2 cup all-purpose flour
- 3 large eggs
- 1/2 tsp salt
- 1 tbsp olive oil (optional)

Instructions:

1. **Prepare the Dough:**
   - On a clean work surface, combine the whole wheat flour and all-purpose flour, making a well in the center. Crack the eggs into the well and add the salt and olive oil (if using).

2. **Mix the Ingredients:**
   - Using a fork, gently beat the eggs, gradually incorporating the flour from the edges of the well until a dough begins to form.

3. **Knead the Dough:**
   - Once the dough comes together, knead it with your hands for about 8-10 minutes, until it becomes smooth and elastic. If the dough is too sticky, add a little more flour; if it's too dry, add a few drops of water.

4. **Rest the Dough:**
   - Wrap the dough in plastic wrap and let it rest at room temperature for at least 30 minutes.
5. **Roll and Cut the Pasta:**
   - Divide the dough into four portions. Using a pasta roller attachment on your KitchenAid stand mixer, roll out each portion of dough to your desired thickness. Start with the widest setting and gradually work down to the thinner settings.
   - Cut the rolled dough into your desired pasta shape (e.g., fettuccine, tagliatelle).
6. **Cook the Pasta:**
   - Bring a large pot of salted water to a boil. Add the fresh pasta and cook for 3-5 minutes, or until al dente.
7. **Serve:**
   - Drain the pasta and serve with your favorite sauce.

Nutritional Information (per serving):
- Calories: 240
- Carbohydrates: 44g
- Protein: 10g
- Fat: 4g
- Fiber: 5g
- Sugar: 2g
- Sodium: 150mg

Tips:

- Whole wheat pasta pairs well with hearty sauces like marinara or Bolognese.
- For a smoother texture, use a mix of whole wheat and all-purpose flour.
- Fresh whole wheat pasta can be dried and stored for later use.

Gluten-Free Pasta

Prep Time: 20 minutes
Cook Time: 3-5 minutes
Servings: 4 servings

Ingredients:

- 2 cups gluten-free all-purpose flour blend
- 1 tsp xanthan gum (if not included in your flour blend)
- 3 large eggs
- 1/2 tsp salt
- 1 tbsp olive oil (optional)

Instructions:

1. **Prepare the Dough:**
   - On a clean work surface, mound the gluten-free flour and make a well in the center. Crack the eggs into the well and add the salt and olive oil (if using). If your flour blend does not contain xanthan gum, add it to the flour.
2. **Mix the Ingredients:**
   - Using a fork, gently beat the eggs, gradually incorporating the flour from the edges of the well until a dough begins to form.
3. **Knead the Dough:**
   - Once the dough comes together, knead it with your hands for about 5-7 minutes, until it becomes smooth and elastic. If the dough

is too sticky, add a little more flour; if it's too dry, add a few drops of water.

4. **Rest the Dough:**
   o Wrap the dough in plastic wrap and let it rest at room temperature for at least 30 minutes.

5. **Roll and Cut the Pasta:**
   o Divide the dough into four portions. Using a pasta roller attachment on your KitchenAid stand mixer, roll out each portion of dough to your desired thickness. Start with the widest setting and gradually work down to the thinner settings.
   o Cut the rolled dough into your desired pasta shape (e.g., fettuccine, tagliatelle).

6. **Cook the Pasta:**
   o Bring a large pot of salted water to a boil. Add the fresh pasta and cook for 3-5 minutes, or until al dente.

7. **Serve:**
   o Drain the pasta and serve with your favorite sauce.

Nutritional Information (per serving):
- Calories: 220
- Carbohydrates: 42g
- Protein: 6g
- Fat: 4g
- Fiber: 3g
- Sugar: 1g

- Sodium: 150mg

Tips:
- Ensure your gluten-free flour blend is suitable for pasta making. A blend with a mix of rice flour, potato starch, and tapioca flour works well.
- Gluten-free pasta tends to cook faster than regular pasta, so keep an eye on it to avoid overcooking.
- Fresh gluten-free pasta can be dried and stored for later use.

Ravioli with Ricotta Filling

Prep Time: 40 minutes
Cook Time: 3-5 minutes
Servings: 4 servings

Ingredients:

For the Pasta Dough:

- 2 cups all-purpose flour
- 3 large eggs
- 1/2 tsp salt
- 1 tbsp olive oil (optional)

For the Filling:

- 1 cup ricotta cheese
- 1/4 cup grated Parmesan cheese
- 1 large egg yolk
- 1 tbsp chopped fresh parsley
- Salt and pepper to taste

Instructions:

1. **Prepare the Dough:**
   - On a clean work surface, mound the flour and make a well in the center. Crack the eggs into the well and add the salt and olive oil (if using).

2. **Mix the Ingredients:**
   - Using a fork, gently beat the eggs, gradually incorporating the flour from the edges of the well until a dough begins to form.

3. **Knead the Dough:**
   - Once the dough comes together, knead it with your hands for about 8-10 minutes, until it becomes smooth and elastic. If the dough is too sticky, add a little more flour; if it's too dry, add a few drops of water.
4. **Rest the Dough:**
   - Wrap the dough in plastic wrap and let it rest at room temperature for at least 30 minutes.
5. **Prepare the Filling:**
   - In a medium bowl, combine the ricotta, Parmesan, egg yolk, parsley, salt, and pepper. Mix until well combined.
6. **Roll the Dough:**
   - Divide the dough into four portions. Using a pasta roller attachment on your KitchenAid stand mixer, roll out each portion of dough to your desired thickness. Start with the widest setting and gradually work down to the thinner settings.
7. **Fill the Ravioli:**
   - Lay one sheet of pasta on a floured surface. Place teaspoonfuls of the ricotta filling evenly spaced apart on the dough. Cover with a second sheet of pasta and press around each mound of filling to seal the edges. Use a ravioli cutter or knife to cut out the ravioli.

8. **Cook the Ravioli:**
   - Bring a large pot of salted water to a boil. Add the ravioli and cook for 3-5 minutes, or until they float to the top.
9. **Serve:**
   - Drain the ravioli and serve with your favorite sauce.

Nutritional Information (per serving):
- Calories: 350
- Carbohydrates: 45g
- Protein: 15g
- Fat: 12g
- Fiber: 2g
- Sugar: 2g
- Sodium: 300mg

Tips:
- Ensure the edges of the ravioli are well-sealed to prevent the filling from leaking out during cooking.
- Use a ravioli mold or tray for uniform and professional-looking ravioli.
- Serve with a simple tomato sauce or browned butter and sage for a delicious meal.

Fettuccine Alfredo

Prep Time: 10 minutes
Cook Time: 10 minutes
Servings: 4 servings
Ingredients:
- 12 oz fettuccine pasta
- 1 cup heavy cream
- 1/2 cup unsalted butter
- 1 cup grated Parmesan cheese
- Salt and pepper to taste
- Fresh parsley, chopped (optional, for garnish)

Instructions:
1. **Cook the Pasta:**
   o Bring a large pot of salted water to a boil. Add the fettuccine pasta and cook according to the package instructions until al dente. Reserve 1 cup of pasta water, then drain the pasta.
2. **Prepare the Alfredo Sauce:**
   o In a large skillet over medium heat, melt the butter. Add the heavy cream and bring to a simmer.
3. **Add the Cheese:**
   o Gradually whisk in the grated Parmesan cheese until the sauce is smooth and creamy.
4. **Combine with Pasta:**
   o Add the cooked fettuccine to the skillet, tossing to coat the pasta evenly with the

sauce. If the sauce is too thick, add the reserved pasta water, a little at a time, until the desired consistency is reached.

5. **Season and Serve:**
   o Season with salt and pepper to taste. Serve immediately, garnished with chopped fresh parsley if desired.

Nutritional Information (per serving):
- Calories: 550
- Carbohydrates: 50g
- Protein: 15g
- Fat: 35g
- Fiber: 2g
- Sugar: 2g
- Sodium: 400mg

Tips:
- Use freshly grated Parmesan cheese for the best flavor and texture.
- For a lighter version, substitute half-and-half for the heavy cream.
- Add grilled chicken or shrimp for a heartier meal.

Spaghetti Carbonara

Prep Time: 10 minutes
Cook Time: 15 minutes
Servings: 4 servings
Ingredients:
- 12 oz spaghetti
- 4 oz pancetta or guanciale, diced
- 2 large eggs
- 1 cup grated Pecorino Romano cheese
- 1 tsp black pepper, freshly ground
- 2 cloves garlic, peeled (optional)
- Salt to taste
- Fresh parsley, chopped (optional, for garnish)

Instructions:
1. **Cook the Spaghetti:**
   - Bring a large pot of salted water to a boil. Add the spaghetti and cook until al dente according to package instructions. Reserve 1 cup of pasta water, then drain the pasta.
2. **Cook the Pancetta:**
   - In a large skillet over medium heat, cook the pancetta (or guanciale) until crispy. If using garlic, add it to the skillet and cook until fragrant, then remove it.
3. **Prepare the Sauce:**
   - In a bowl, whisk together the eggs, grated Pecorino Romano cheese, and black pepper.

4. **Combine Pasta and Pancetta:**
   o Add the cooked spaghetti to the skillet with the pancetta. Remove the skillet from heat.
5. **Add the Sauce:**
   o Quickly pour the egg and cheese mixture over the pasta, tossing continuously to create a creamy sauce. Add reserved pasta water, a little at a time, until the desired consistency is reached.
6. **Season and Serve:**
   o Season with additional black pepper and salt to taste. Serve immediately, garnished with chopped fresh parsley if desired.

Nutritional Information (per serving):
- Calories: 500
- Carbohydrates: 55g
- Protein: 20g
- Fat: 20g
- Fiber: 3g
- Sugar: 2g
- Sodium: 600mg

Tips:
- Work quickly when adding the egg mixture to avoid scrambling the eggs.
- Use freshly grated Pecorino Romano for the best flavor.
- Serve with a simple green salad or garlic bread.

Pappardelle with Bolognese

Prep Time: 20 minutes
Cook Time: 2 hours
Servings: 4 servings
Ingredients:
For the Pasta:
- 2 cups all-purpose flour
- 3 large eggs
- 1/2 tsp salt

For the Bolognese Sauce:
- 2 tbsp olive oil
- 1 onion, finely chopped
- 2 carrots, finely chopped
- 2 celery stalks, finely chopped
- 2 cloves garlic, minced
- 1 lb ground beef
- 1/2 lb ground pork
- 1 cup whole milk
- 1 cup dry white wine
- 1 can (28 oz) crushed tomatoes
- 1 bay leaf
- Salt and pepper to taste
- Fresh basil or parsley, chopped (optional, for garnish)

Instructions:

1. **Prepare the Pasta Dough:**
   o On a clean work surface, mound the flour and make a well in the center. Crack the eggs into the well and add the salt.

- Using a fork, gently beat the eggs, gradually incorporating the flour from the edges of the well until a dough begins to form.
- Knead the dough for about 8-10 minutes, until it becomes smooth and elastic. Wrap the dough in plastic wrap and let it rest at room temperature for at least 30 minutes.

2. **Make the Bolognese Sauce:**
   - Heat the olive oil in a large pot over medium heat. Add the onion, carrots, and celery and cook until softened, about 10 minutes.
   - Add the garlic and cook for another minute.
   - Add the ground beef and pork, breaking it up with a spoon, and cook until browned.
   - Pour in the milk and simmer until it has evaporated, then add the wine and simmer until it has evaporated.
   - Stir in the crushed tomatoes and bay leaf. Reduce the heat to low and let the sauce simmer for 1 1/2 to 2 hours, stirring occasionally. Season with salt and pepper to taste.

3. **Roll and Cut the Pasta:**
   - Divide the dough into four portions. Using a pasta roller attachment on your KitchenAid stand mixer, roll out each portion of dough to your desired thickness. Start with the widest setting and gradually work down to the thinner settings.

- Cut the rolled dough into wide ribbons to make pappardelle.
4. **Cook the Pasta:**
   - Bring a large pot of salted water to a boil. Add the pappardelle and cook for 3-5 minutes, or until al dente.
5. **Combine and Serve:**
   - Drain the pasta and toss it with the Bolognese sauce. Serve immediately, garnished with chopped fresh basil or parsley if desired.

Nutritional Information (per serving):
- Calories: 700
- Carbohydrates: 60g
- Protein: 35g
- Fat: 35g
- Fiber: 5g
- Sugar: 10g
- Sodium: 800mg

Tips:
- For a richer flavor, let the Bolognese sauce simmer for an additional hour.
- Use fresh, high-quality ingredients for the best results.
- Serve with grated Parmesan cheese and a side of crusty bread.

Lasagna Sheets

Prep Time: 20 minutes
Cook Time: 3-5 minutes
Servings: Makes enough sheets for a 9x13 inch lasagna
Ingredients:

- 2 cups all-purpose flour
- 3 large eggs
- 1/2 tsp salt
- 1 tbsp olive oil (optional)

Instructions:

1. **Prepare the Dough:** On a clean work surface, mound the flour and make a well in the center. Crack the eggs into the well and add the salt and olive oil (if using).

2. **Mix the Ingredients:**
   o Using a fork, gently beat the eggs, gradually incorporating the flour from the edges of the well until a dough begins to form.

3. **Knead the Dough:**
   o Once the dough comes together, knead it with your hands for about 8-10 minutes, until it becomes smooth and elastic. If the dough is too sticky, add a little more flour; if it's too dry, add a few drops of water.

4. **Rest the Dough:**
   o Wrap the dough in plastic wrap and let it rest at room temperature for at least 30 minutes.

5. **Roll the Dough:**

o Divide the dough into four portions. Using a pasta roller attachment on your KitchenAid stand mixer, roll out each portion of dough to your desired thickness. Start with the widest setting and gradually work down to the thinner settings.

6. **Cut the Sheets:** Cut the rolled dough into rectangular sheets to fit your lasagna pan (typically 9x13 inches).

7. **Cook the Sheets:**
   o Bring a large pot of salted water to a boil. Add the lasagna sheets a few at a time and cook for 3-5 minutes, or until al dente.

8. **Use in Lasagna:** Drain the sheets and use them immediately in your favorite lasagna recipe.

Nutritional Information (per serving):
- Calories: 220
- Carbohydrates: 42g
- Protein: 8g
- Fat: 4g
- Fiber: 2g
- Sugar: 1g
- Sodium: 150mg

Tips:
- Lay cooked sheets on a clean kitchen towel to dry slightly before assembling your lasagna.
- Fresh lasagna sheets can be layered without pre-cooking if using enough sauce.
- Use fresh, high-quality ingredients for the best results.

Gnocchi

Prep Time: 1 hour
Cook Time: 5 minutes
Servings: 4 servings

Ingredients:

- 2 pounds russet potatoes
- 1 cup all-purpose flour, plus more for dusting
- 1 large egg, lightly beaten
- 1 tsp salt

Instructions:

1. **Cook the Potatoes:**
   - Preheat your oven to 400°F (200°C). Bake the potatoes for 45-60 minutes, or until tender. Let them cool slightly, then peel and pass them through a potato ricer or mash them until smooth.

2. **Prepare the Dough:**
   - On a clean work surface, mound the riced potatoes and make a well in the center. Add the flour, beaten egg, and salt.

3. **Mix the Ingredients:**
   - Using your hands, gently mix the ingredients together, gradually incorporating the flour until a dough forms. Be careful not to overwork the dough to avoid tough gnocchi.

4. **Shape the Gnocchi:**

- Divide the dough into four portions. Roll each portion into a long rope about 1/2 inch thick. Cut the rope into 1-inch pieces.

5. **Form the Gnocchi:**
   - Using a fork or a gnocchi board, gently press each piece of dough to create ridges.

6. **Cook the Gnocchi:**
   - Bring a large pot of salted water to a boil. Add the gnocchi in batches and cook until they float to the surface, about 2-3 minutes.

7. **Serve:**
   - Remove the gnocchi with a slotted spoon and serve with your favorite sauce.

Nutritional Information (per serving):
- Calories: 250
- Carbohydrates: 50g
- Protein: 7g
- Fat: 2g
- Fiber: 4g
- Sugar: 2g
- Sodium: 300mg

Tips:
- Use russet potatoes for the best texture.
- Do not overmix the dough to keep the gnocchi light and fluffy.
- Serve with a simple tomato sauce, pesto, or browned butter and sage.

DOUGHS

Pizza Dough

Prep Time: 15 minutes (plus 1-2 hours rising time)
Cook Time: 10-15 minutes
Servings: Makes 2 12-inch pizzas

Ingredients:

- 3 1/2 to 4 cups all-purpose flour
- 1 packet (2 1/4 tsp) active dry yeast
- 1 1/2 cups warm water (110°F)
- 2 tbsp olive oil
- 2 tsp salt
- 1 tsp sugar

Instructions:

1. **Activate the Yeast:**
   - In a small bowl, combine warm water, sugar, and yeast. Let it sit for about 5-10 minutes, or until frothy.

2. **Mix the Dough:**
   - In the bowl of your KitchenAid stand mixer, combine 3 1/2 cups of flour and salt. Attach the dough hook.
   - Add the yeast mixture and olive oil to the flour mixture.
   - Mix on low speed until the dough begins to come together. Gradually increase the speed to medium and knead for about 5-7 minutes,

until the dough is smooth and elastic. If the dough is too sticky, add more flour, 1 tablespoon at a time.

3. **First Rise:**
   - Transfer the dough to a lightly greased bowl. Cover it with a clean kitchen towel.
   - Let it rise in a warm, draft-free area for 1-2 hours, or until doubled in size.

4. **Shape the Dough:**
   - Punch down the dough to release any air bubbles. Divide the dough in half.
   - On a lightly floured surface, roll out each portion into a 12-inch circle.

5. **Bake the Pizza:**
   - Preheat your oven to 475°F (245°C) with a pizza stone or baking sheet inside.
   - Transfer the rolled-out dough to a piece of parchment paper. Add your desired toppings.
   - Carefully slide the pizza onto the preheated stone or baking sheet. Bake for 10-15 minutes, or until the crust is golden and the cheese is bubbly.

Nutritional Information (per slice):
- Calories: 140
- Carbohydrates: 27g
- Protein: 4g
- Fat: 2g
- Fiber: 1g

- Sugar: 1g
- Sodium: 250mg

Tips:

- For a crispier crust, pre-bake the dough for 5 minutes before adding toppings.
- Store any unused dough in the refrigerator for up to 3 days or freeze for up to 3 months.
- Use high-quality ingredients for the best pizza.

Calzone Dough

Prep Time: 15 minutes (plus 1-2 hours rising time)
Cook Time: 15-20 minutes
Servings: Makes 4 calzones

Ingredients:
- 3 1/2 to 4 cups all-purpose flour
- 1 packet (2 1/4 tsp) active dry yeast
- 1 1/2 cups warm water (110°F)
- 2 tbsp olive oil
- 2 tsp salt
- 1 tsp sugar

Instructions:
1. **Activate the Yeast:**
   - In a small bowl, combine warm water, sugar, and yeast. Let it sit for about 5-10 minutes, or until frothy.
2. **Mix the Dough:**
   - In the bowl of your KitchenAid stand mixer, combine 3 1/2 cups of flour and salt. Attach the dough hook.
   - Add the yeast mixture and olive oil to the flour mixture.
   - Mix on low speed until the dough begins to come together. Gradually increase the speed to medium and knead for about 5-7 minutes, until the dough is smooth and elastic. If the dough is too sticky, add more flour, 1 tablespoon at a time.

3. **First Rise:**
   - Transfer the dough to a lightly greased bowl. Cover it with a clean kitchen towel.
   - Let it rise in a warm, draft-free area for 1-2 hours, or until doubled in size.
4. **Shape the Dough:**
   - Punch down the dough to release any air bubbles. Divide the dough into four equal portions.
   - On a lightly floured surface, roll out each portion into a 6-8 inch circle.
5. **Fill and Seal:**
   - Place your desired fillings on one half of each dough circle, leaving a 1-inch border. Fold the dough over the filling and press the edges to seal. Use a fork to crimp the edges.
6. **Bake the Calzones:**
   - Preheat your oven to 400°F (200°C). Place the calzones on a baking sheet lined with parchment paper.
   - Cut a few small slits in the top of each calzone to allow steam to escape.
   - Bake for 15-20 minutes, or until golden brown.

Nutritional Information (per calzone):
- Calories: 300
- Carbohydrates: 54g
- Protein: 8g
- Fat: 7g

- Fiber: 2g
- Sugar: 2g
- Sodium: 500mg

Tips:

- Brush the tops of the calzones with olive oil or an egg wash for a golden finish.
- Experiment with different fillings such as cheese, meats, and vegetables.
- Serve with marinara sauce for dipping.

Pretzel Dough

Prep Time: 20 minutes (plus 1 hour rising time)
Cook Time: 12-15 minutes
Servings: Makes 8 pretzels

Ingredients:
- 4 cups all-purpose flour
- 1 packet (2 1/4 tsp) active dry yeast
- 1 1/2 cups warm water (110°F)
- 1 tbsp sugar
- 2 tsp salt
- 1/4 cup baking soda
- 1 large egg, beaten (for egg wash)
- Coarse sea salt (for topping)

Instructions:
1. **Activate the Yeast:**
   - In a small bowl, combine warm water and sugar. Sprinkle the yeast over the water and let it sit for about 5-10 minutes, or until frothy.
2. **Mix the Dough:**
   - In the bowl of your KitchenAid stand mixer, combine the flour and salt. Attach the dough hook.
   - Add the yeast mixture to the flour mixture.
   - Mix on low speed until the dough begins to come together. Gradually increase the speed to medium and knead for about 5-7 minutes, until the dough is smooth and elastic.

3. **First Rise:**
    o Transfer the dough to a lightly greased bowl. Cover it with a clean kitchen towel.
    o Let it rise in a warm, draft-free area for about 1 hour, or until doubled in size.
4. **Shape the Pretzels:**
    o Preheat your oven to 450°F (230°C). Line a baking sheet with parchment paper.
    o Punch down the dough and divide it into 8 equal pieces. Roll each piece into a long rope and shape it into a pretzel.
5. **Prepare the Baking Soda Bath:**
    o In a large pot, bring 10 cups of water and the baking soda to a boil. Carefully dip each pretzel into the boiling water for about 30 seconds, then remove with a slotted spoon and place on the prepared baking sheet.
6. **Bake the Pretzels:**
    o Brush each pretzel with the beaten egg and sprinkle with coarse sea salt.
    o Bake for 12-15 minutes, or until golden brown.

Nutritional Information (per pretzel):
- Calories: 210
- Carbohydrates: 42g
- Protein: 6g
- Fat: 2g
- Fiber: 2g
- Sugar: 1g

- Sodium: 400mg

Tips:

- For a sweeter variation, roll the pretzels in cinnamon sugar after baking.
- Serve with mustard or cheese sauce for dipping.
- Use parchment paper to prevent sticking and make cleanup easier.

Empanada Dough

Prep Time: 15 minutes (plus chilling time)
Cook Time: 20-25 minutes
Servings: Makes 12-15 empanadas
Ingredients:
- 2 1/2 cups all-purpose flour
- 1/2 tsp salt
- 1/2 cup unsalted butter, chilled and cubed
- 1 large egg
- 1/3 cup ice water
- 1 tbsp white vinegar

Instructions:
1. **Mix the Dry Ingredients:**
   - In the bowl of your KitchenAid stand mixer, combine the flour and salt.
2. **Add the Butter:**
   - Add the chilled, cubed butter to the flour mixture. Use the paddle attachment to mix on low speed until the mixture resembles coarse crumbs.
3. **Combine Wet Ingredients:**
   - In a small bowl, whisk together the egg, ice water, and vinegar.
4. **Form the Dough:**
   - Gradually add the wet ingredients to the flour mixture, mixing on low speed until the dough comes together.

- Turn the dough out onto a lightly floured surface and knead gently to form a smooth ball.

5. **Chill the Dough:**
   - Wrap the dough in plastic wrap and refrigerate for at least 1 hour before using.

6. **Roll and Cut the Dough:**
   - Preheat your oven to 375°F (190°C). Line a baking sheet with parchment paper.
   - Roll out the chilled dough on a lightly floured surface to about 1/8 inch thickness.
   - Use a round cutter to cut out circles of dough (about 4-5 inches in diameter).

7. **Fill and Seal:**
   - Place your desired filling in the center of each dough circle. Fold the dough over to form a half-moon shape and press the edges to seal. Use a fork to crimp the edges.

8. **Bake the Empanadas:**
   - Place the empanadas on the prepared baking sheet. Brush the tops with a beaten egg.
   - Bake for 20-25 minutes, or until golden brown.

Nutritional Information (per empanada):
- Calories: 180
- Carbohydrates: 18g
- Protein: 4g
- Fat: 10g
- Fiber: 1g

- Sugar: 0g
- Sodium: 150mg

Tips:
- Ensure the butter is very cold to create a flaky dough.
- Experiment with different fillings such as beef, chicken, cheese, or vegetables.
- Empanadas can be frozen before baking and baked directly from the freezer.

Tortilla Dough

Prep Time: 20 minutes (plus resting time)
Cook Time: 2-3 minutes per tortilla
Servings: Makes 12 tortillas
Ingredients:
- 2 cups all-purpose flour
- 1/2 tsp salt
- 1/2 tsp baking powder
- 1/4 cup vegetable oil
- 3/4 cup warm water

Instructions:
1. **Mix Dry Ingredients:**
   - In a large bowl, combine the flour, salt, and baking powder.
2. **Add Wet Ingredients:**
   - Add the vegetable oil and warm water to the dry ingredients. Mix until the dough comes together.
3. **Knead the Dough:**
   - Turn the dough out onto a lightly floured surface and knead for about 5 minutes, until smooth and elastic.
4. **Rest the Dough:**
   - Divide the dough into 12 equal pieces and shape each piece into a ball. Cover with a damp cloth and let rest for 15 minutes.
5. **Roll the Tortillas:**

- On a lightly floured surface, roll out each ball of dough into a thin circle, about 8 inches in diameter.

6. **Cook the Tortillas:**
   - Preheat a skillet or griddle over medium-high heat. Cook each tortilla for about 1-2 minutes on each side, until golden brown spots appear.

7. **Serve:**
   - Stack the cooked tortillas and keep them warm in a clean kitchen towel until ready to serve.

Nutritional Information (per tortilla):
- Calories: 110
- Carbohydrates: 17g
- Protein: 2g
- Fat: 3g
- Fiber: 1g
- Sugar: 0g
- Sodium: 100mg

Tips:
- For a softer tortilla, add a little more water if the dough feels too dry.
- Use a rolling pin to get the tortillas as thin as possible.
- Tortillas can be stored in an airtight container for up to 3 days or frozen for up to 3 months.

Pita Bread Dough

Prep Time: 20 minutes (plus 1 hour rising time)
Cook Time: 10 minutes
Servings: Makes 8 pitas
Ingredients:
- 3 cups all-purpose flour
- 1 packet (2 1/4 tsp) active dry yeast
- 1 cup warm water (110°F)
- 2 tbsp olive oil
- 1 tsp salt
- 1 tsp sugar

Instructions:
1. **Activate the Yeast:**
   - In a small bowl, combine warm water, sugar, and yeast. Let it sit for about 5-10 minutes, or until frothy.
2. **Mix the Dough:**
   - In the bowl of your KitchenAid stand mixer, combine the flour and salt. Attach the dough hook.
   - Add the yeast mixture and olive oil to the flour mixture.
   - Mix on low speed until the dough begins to come together. Gradually increase the speed to medium and knead for about 5-7 minutes, until the dough is smooth and elastic.
3. **First Rise:**

- o Transfer the dough to a lightly greased bowl. Cover it with a clean kitchen towel.
- o Let it rise in a warm, draft-free area for about 1 hour, or until doubled in size.

4. **Shape the Dough:**
   - o Punch down the dough to release any air bubbles. Divide the dough into 8 equal pieces.
   - o On a lightly floured surface, roll out each piece into a 6-inch circle.

5. **Bake the Pitas:**
   - o Preheat your oven to 475°F (245°C) and place a baking stone or baking sheet inside to heat.
   - o Place the rolled-out dough circles onto the preheated stone or baking sheet. Bake for 8-10 minutes, or until the pitas puff up and are lightly browned.

6. **Serve:**
   - o Remove the pitas from the oven and let them cool slightly. Serve warm or at room temperature.

Nutritional Information (per pita):
- Calories: 170
- Carbohydrates: 30g
- Protein: 5g
- Fat: 3g
- Fiber: 1g
- Sugar: 0g

- Sodium: 250mg

Tips:

- Ensure your oven and baking stone/sheet are fully preheated for the best puffing.
- For softer pitas, cover them with a clean kitchen towel as they cool.
- Store pitas in an airtight container for up to 3 days or freeze for up to 3 months.

Naan Bread Dough

Prep Time: 20 minutes (plus 1 hour rising time)
Cook Time: 2-3 minutes per naan
Servings: Makes 8 naan

Ingredients:

- 3 cups all-purpose flour
- 1 packet (2 1/4 tsp) active dry yeast
- 1/2 cup warm water (110°F)
- 1/4 cup plain yogurt
- 1/4 cup milk
- 2 tbsp olive oil
- 1 tsp salt
- 1 tsp sugar

Instructions:

1. **Activate the Yeast:**
   - In a small bowl, combine warm water, sugar, and yeast. Let it sit for about 5-10 minutes, or until frothy.

2. **Mix the Dough:**
   - In the bowl of your KitchenAid stand mixer, combine the flour and salt. Attach the dough hook.
   - Add the yeast mixture, yogurt, milk, and olive oil to the flour mixture.
   - Mix on low speed until the dough begins to come together. Gradually increase the speed to medium and knead for about 5-7 minutes, until the dough is smooth and elastic.

3. **First Rise:**

- Transfer the dough to a lightly greased bowl. Cover it with a clean kitchen towel.
- Let it rise in a warm, draft-free area for about 1 hour, or until doubled in size.

4. **Shape the Dough:**
   - Punch down the dough to release any air bubbles. Divide the dough into 8 equal pieces.
   - On a lightly floured surface, roll out each piece into an oval shape, about 1/4 inch thick.
5. **Cook the Naan:** Preheat a skillet or griddle over medium-high heat. Cook each naan for about 1-2 minutes on each side, until bubbles form and the naan is golden brown.
6. **Serve:** Brush the naan with melted butter or ghee and serve warm.

Nutritional Information (per naan):
- Calories: 200
- Carbohydrates: 35g
- Protein: 5g
- Fat: 4g
- Fiber: 1g
- Sugar: 1g
- Sodium: 300mg

Tips:
- For garlic naan, brush with melted butter and minced garlic after cooking.
- Use a cast-iron skillet for the best results.
- Store naan in an airtight container for up to 3 days or freeze for up to 3 months.

Cinnamon Roll Dough

Prep Time: 20 minutes (plus 1-2 hours rising time)
Cook Time: 25-30 minutes
Servings: Makes 12 rolls
Ingredients:
For the Dough:
- 4 cups all-purpose flour
- 1 packet (2 1/4 tsp) active dry yeast
- 1 cup warm milk (110°F)
- 1/4 cup granulated sugar
- 1/4 cup unsalted butter, melted
- 1 tsp salt
- 2 large eggs

For the Filling:
- 1/2 cup unsalted butter, softened
- 1 cup brown sugar, packed
- 2 tbsp ground cinnamon

For the Frosting:
- 4 oz cream cheese, softened
- 1/4 cup unsalted butter, softened
- 1 1/2 cups powdered sugar
- 1 tsp vanilla extract

Instructions:
1. **Activate the Yeast:**
    - In a small bowl, combine warm milk and sugar. Sprinkle the yeast over the milk and let it sit for about 5-10 minutes, or until frothy.

2. **Mix the Dough:**
   - In the bowl of your KitchenAid stand mixer, combine the flour and salt. Attach the dough hook.
   - Add the yeast mixture, melted butter, and eggs to the flour mixture.
   - Mix on low speed until the dough begins to come together. Gradually increase the speed to medium and knead for about 5-7 minutes, until the dough is smooth and elastic.

3. **First Rise:**
   - Transfer the dough to a lightly greased bowl. Cover it with a clean kitchen towel.
   - Let it rise in a warm, draft-free area for 1-2 hours, or until doubled in size.

4. **Prepare the Filling:**
   - In a small bowl, mix together the softened butter, brown sugar, and ground cinnamon until well combined.

5. **Shape the Rolls:**
   - Punch down the dough to release any air bubbles. Roll out the dough on a lightly floured surface into a rectangle, about 16x12 inches.
   - Spread the filling mixture evenly over the dough. Starting from the long side, roll the dough into a tight log. Cut the log into 12 equal pieces.

6. **Second Rise:**

- Place the rolls in a greased 9x13 inch baking dish. Cover with a clean kitchen towel and let them rise for about 30-45 minutes, or until doubled in size.

7. **Bake the Rolls:**
   - Preheat your oven to 350°F (175°C). Bake the rolls for 25-30 minutes, or until golden brown.

8. **Prepare the Frosting:**
   - In a medium bowl, beat the cream cheese and butter until smooth. Add the powdered sugar and vanilla extract, and mix until well combined.

9. **Frost the Rolls:** Spread the frosting over the warm cinnamon rolls before serving.

Nutritional Information (per roll):
- Calories: 450
- Carbohydrates: 68g
- Protein: 7g
- Fat: 17g
- Fiber: 2g
- Sugar: 38g
- Sodium: 350mg

Tips:
- For an extra gooey filling, add 1/4 cup of maple syrup to the filling mixture.
- Serve the rolls warm for the best flavor and texture.
- Store leftover rolls in an airtight container at room temperature for up to 2 days, or refrigerate for up to a week.

Donut Dough

Prep Time: 20 minutes (plus 1-2 hours rising time)
Cook Time: 2-3 minutes per donut
Servings: Makes 12 donuts

Ingredients:

- 3 1/2 cups all-purpose flour
- 1 packet (2 1/4 tsp) active dry yeast
- 1 cup warm milk (110°F)
- 1/4 cup granulated sugar
- 1/4 cup unsalted butter, melted
- 1 tsp salt
- 2 large eggs
- Vegetable oil, for frying

For the Glaze:

- 2 cups powdered sugar
- 1/4 cup milk
- 1 tsp vanilla extract

Instructions:

1. **Activate the Yeast:**
   - In a small bowl, combine warm milk and sugar. Sprinkle the yeast over the milk and let it sit for about 5-10 minutes, or until frothy.
2. **Mix the Dough:**
   - In the bowl of your KitchenAid stand mixer, combine the flour and salt. Attach the dough hook.

- Add the yeast mixture, melted butter, and eggs to the flour mixture.
- Mix on low speed until the dough begins to come together. Gradually increase the speed to medium and knead for about 5-7 minutes, until the dough is smooth and elastic.

3. **First Rise:**
   - Transfer the dough to a lightly greased bowl. Cover it with a clean kitchen towel.
   - Let it rise in a warm, draft-free area for 1-2 hours, or until doubled in size.

4. **Shape the Donuts:**
   - Punch down the dough to release any air bubbles. Roll out the dough on a lightly floured surface to about 1/2 inch thickness.
   - Use a donut cutter or two round cutters (one large and one small) to cut out the donuts and holes.

5. **Second Rise:**
   - Place the donuts and holes on a lightly floured baking sheet. Cover with a clean kitchen towel and let them rise for about 30 minutes, or until slightly puffed.

6. **Fry the Donuts:**
   - Heat vegetable oil in a deep fryer or large pot to 350°F (175°C). Fry the donuts in batches for about 2-3 minutes per side, or until golden brown.

- o Remove the donuts with a slotted spoon and drain on paper towels.
7. **Prepare the Glaze:**
   - o In a medium bowl, whisk together the powdered sugar, milk, and vanilla extract until smooth.
8. **Glaze the Donuts:**
   - o Dip the warm donuts into the glaze, allowing any excess to drip off. Place the glazed donuts on a wire rack to set.

Nutritional Information (per donut):
- Calories: 350
- Carbohydrates: 55g
- Protein: 6g
- Fat: 12g
- Fiber: 2g
- Sugar: 25g
- Sodium: 300mg

Tips:
- For a different flavor, dip the donuts in cinnamon sugar instead of glaze.
- Add a few drops of food coloring to the glaze for festive donuts.
- Store leftover donuts in an airtight container at room temperature for up to 2 days.

Croissant Dough

Prep Time: 1 hour (plus overnight chilling and several resting periods)
Cook Time: 15-20 minutes
Servings: Makes 12 croissants

Ingredients:
- 4 cups all-purpose flour
- 1 packet (2 1/4 tsp) active dry yeast
- 1 cup warm milk (110°F)
- 1/4 cup granulated sugar
- 2 tsp salt
- 1/4 cup unsalted butter, melted
- 1 cup unsalted butter, cold and cubed (for laminating)

Instructions:
1. **Activate the Yeast:**
    - In a small bowl, combine warm milk and sugar. Sprinkle the yeast over the milk and let it sit for about 5-10 minutes, or until frothy.
2. **Mix the Dough:**
    - In the bowl of your KitchenAid stand mixer, combine the flour and salt. Attach the dough hook.
    - Add the yeast mixture and melted butter to the flour mixture.
    - Mix on low speed until the dough begins to come together. Gradually increase the speed

to medium and knead for about 5-7 minutes, until the dough is smooth and elastic.

3. **First Rise:**
   - Transfer the dough to a lightly greased bowl. Cover it with a clean kitchen towel.
   - Let it rise in a warm, draft-free area for about 1 hour, or until doubled in size.

4. **Prepare the Butter Block:**
   - On a piece of parchment paper, arrange the cold, cubed butter into a 6x6 inch square. Cover with another piece of parchment paper and use a rolling pin to flatten and shape it into an even block. Refrigerate until firm.

5. **Laminate the Dough:**
   - Roll out the dough on a lightly floured surface into a 12x12 inch square. Place the butter block in the center and fold the corners of the dough over the butter, encasing it completely.
   - Roll out the dough into a 20x10 inch rectangle. Fold the dough into thirds like a letter, then wrap it in plastic wrap and refrigerate for 30 minutes.
   - Repeat the rolling and folding process two more times, refrigerating for 30 minutes between each turn.

6. **Shape the Croissants:**

- Roll out the dough into a 24x12 inch rectangle. Cut the dough into 12 triangles. Starting from the base of each triangle, roll the dough up towards the tip, tucking the tip under the croissant.

7. **Final Rise:**
   - Place the croissants on a baking sheet lined with parchment paper. Cover with a clean kitchen towel and let them rise for about 1 hour, or until puffy.

8. **Bake the Croissants:**
   - Preheat your oven to 375°F (190°C). Bake the croissants for 15-20 minutes, or until golden brown.

Nutritional Information (per croissant):
- Calories: 320
- Carbohydrates: 40g
- Protein: 6g
- Fat: 16g
- Fiber: 2g
- Sugar: 6g
- Sodium: 350mg

Tips:
- Ensure the butter stays cold throughout the laminating process to achieve flaky layers.
- Brush the croissants with an egg wash (1 beaten egg with 1 tbsp water) before baking for a shiny finish.
- Serve warm or at room temperature with butter, jam, or chocolate.

DIPS AND SAUCES

Classic Hummus

Prep Time: 10 minutes
Cook Time: 0 minutes
Servings: 4 servings

Ingredients:

- 1 can (15 oz) chickpeas, drained and rinsed
- 1/4 cup tahini
- 2 tbsp extra virgin olive oil
- 1/4 cup lemon juice (about 2 lemons)
- 1-2 cloves garlic, minced
- 1/2 tsp ground cumin
- 1/2 tsp salt
- 2-3 tbsp water (as needed)
- Paprika and olive oil for garnish

Instructions:

1. **Blend the Ingredients:**
   - In a food processor, combine the chickpeas, tahini, olive oil, lemon juice, garlic, cumin, and salt.

2. **Process Until Smooth:**
   - Process the mixture until smooth. Add water, one tablespoon at a time, until the desired consistency is reached.

3. **Adjust Seasoning:**

- Taste and adjust seasoning as needed. Add more salt, lemon juice, or garlic to taste.
4. **Serve:**
   - Transfer the hummus to a serving bowl. Drizzle with olive oil and sprinkle with paprika.

Nutritional Information (per serving):
- Calories: 220
- Carbohydrates: 20g
- Protein: 6g
- Fat: 14g
- Fiber: 5g
- Sugar: 1g
- Sodium: 350mg

Tips:
- For extra smooth hummus, peel the chickpeas before blending.
- Store hummus in an airtight container in the refrigerator for up to 5 days.
- Serve with pita bread, fresh vegetables, or as a spread on sandwiches.

Spinach and Artichoke Dip

Prep Time: 15 minutes
Cook Time: 25 minutes
Servings: 6 servings
Ingredients:
- 1 package (10 oz) frozen chopped spinach, thawed and drained
- 1 can (14 oz) artichoke hearts, drained and chopped
- 1 cup sour cream
- 1 cup mayonnaise
- 1 cup grated Parmesan cheese
- 1 cup shredded mozzarella cheese
- 2 cloves garlic, minced
- Salt and pepper to taste

Instructions:
1. **Preheat the Oven:**
   - Preheat your oven to 375°F (190°C).
2. **Combine the Ingredients:**
   - In a large bowl, mix together the spinach, artichoke hearts, sour cream, mayonnaise, Parmesan cheese, mozzarella cheese, and garlic. Season with salt and pepper.
3. **Bake the Dip:**
   - Transfer the mixture to a baking dish and spread it out evenly. Bake for 25 minutes, or until the top is golden brown and bubbly.
4. Serve warm with chips, bread, or fresh vegetables.

188

Nutritional Information (per serving):

- Calories: 350
- Carbohydrates: 7g
- Protein: 10g
- Fat: 31g
- Fiber: 3g
- Sugar: 2g
- Sodium: 650mg

Tips:

- Use fresh spinach instead of frozen for a fresher flavor.
- Add a pinch of red pepper flakes for a bit of heat.
- Store leftovers in the refrigerator for up to 3 days and reheat before serving.

Guacamole

Prep Time: 10 minutes
Cook Time: 0 minutes
Servings: 4 servings
Ingredients:
- 3 ripe avocados
- 1 lime, juiced
- 1/2 tsp salt
- 1/2 tsp ground cumin
- 1/2 tsp ground cayenne pepper
- 1/2 medium onion, diced
- 2 Roma tomatoes, diced
- 1 tbsp chopped cilantro
- 1 clove garlic, minced

Instructions:
1. **Prepare the Avocados:**
   - Cut the avocados in half, remove the pit, and scoop the flesh into a mixing bowl.
2. **Mash the Avocados:**
   - Mash the avocados with a fork until smooth or slightly chunky, depending on your preference.
3. **Add the Remaining Ingredients:**
   - Add lime juice, salt, cumin, cayenne pepper, onion, tomatoes, cilantro, and garlic. Stir to combine.
4. **Adjust Seasoning:**

- o Taste and adjust seasoning as needed. Add more salt, lime juice, or cayenne pepper to taste.

5. **Serve:**
   - o Serve immediately with tortilla chips, as a topping for tacos, or as a side with any Mexican dish.

Nutritional Information (per serving):
- Calories: 220
- Carbohydrates: 12g
- Protein: 3g
- Fat: 18g
- Fiber: 9g
- Sugar: 2g
- Sodium: 300mg

Tips:
- To keep guacamole from browning, press plastic wrap directly onto the surface of the guacamole before storing in the refrigerator.
- Add diced jalapeño for extra heat.
- Serve with fresh lime wedges for an extra burst of flavor.

Salsa Verde

Prep Time: 10 minutes
Cook Time: 15 minutes
Servings: 4 servings

Ingredients:

- 1 pound tomatillos, husked and rinsed
- 1/2 cup chopped white onion
- 1/2 cup cilantro leaves
- 1 tbsp fresh lime juice
- 1 jalapeño or serrano pepper, chopped (seeds removed for less heat)
- 1 clove garlic, minced
- Salt to taste

Instructions:

1. **Cook the Tomatillos:**
   - Place the tomatillos in a large pot and cover with water. Bring to a boil and cook for 5 minutes, or until the tomatillos are soft. Drain and let cool slightly.

2. **Blend the Ingredients:**
   - In a blender or food processor, combine the cooked tomatillos, onion, cilantro, lime juice, jalapeño, and garlic. Blend until smooth.

3. **Season the Salsa:**
   - Taste and add salt as needed.

4. Serve immediately or refrigerate for later use. Salsa verde can be served with chips, tacos, or as a sauce for meats.

Nutritional Information (per serving):

- Calories: 50
- Carbohydrates: 10g
- Protein: 1g
- Fat: 0g
- Fiber: 2g
- Sugar: 6g
- Sodium: 10mg

Tips:

- For a smoky flavor, roast the tomatillos and jalapeño under the broiler until charred before blending.
- Adjust the heat level by adding more or less jalapeño.
- Store in an airtight container in the refrigerator for up to 1 week.

Marinara Sauce

Prep Time: 10 minutes
Cook Time: 30 minutes
Servings: 4 servings
Ingredients:

- 2 tbsp olive oil
- 1 small onion, finely chopped
- 3 cloves garlic, minced
- 1 can (28 oz) crushed tomatoes
- 1 tsp dried oregano
- 1 tsp dried basil
- 1/2 tsp salt
- 1/4 tsp black pepper
- 1/4 tsp red pepper flakes (optional)
- 1 tbsp chopped fresh basil (optional, for garnish)

Instructions:

1. **Sauté the Aromatics:**
   - Heat the olive oil in a large saucepan over medium heat. Add the onion and cook until softened, about 5 minutes. Add the garlic and cook for an additional minute.
2. **Add the Tomatoes:**
   - Stir in the crushed tomatoes, oregano, dried basil, salt, black pepper, and red pepper flakes (if using).
3. **Simmer the Sauce:**

- Bring the sauce to a simmer. Reduce the heat to low and let it simmer for 20-30 minutes, stirring occasionally.

4. **Adjust Seasoning:**
   - Taste and adjust seasoning as needed. Add more salt, pepper, or herbs to taste.

5. **Serve:**
   - Serve the marinara sauce over pasta, as a pizza sauce, or as a dip for breadsticks. Garnish with fresh basil if desired.

Nutritional Information (per serving):
- Calories: 120
- Carbohydrates: 14g
- Protein: 2g
- Fat: 7g
- Fiber: 4g
- Sugar: 8g
- Sodium: 400mg

Tips:
- For a smoother sauce, blend with an immersion blender.
- Add a splash of red wine for extra depth of flavor.
- Store in an airtight container in the refrigerator for up to 5 days or freeze for up to 3 months.

Alfredo Sauce

Prep Time: 5 minutes
Cook Time: 10 minutes
Servings: 4 servings
Ingredients:

- 1/2 cup unsalted butter
- 1 cup heavy cream
- 1 1/2 cups grated Parmesan cheese
- 2 cloves garlic, minced
- 1/2 tsp salt
- 1/4 tsp black pepper
- 1/4 tsp ground nutmeg (optional)
- Fresh parsley, chopped (optional, for garnish)

Instructions:

1. **Melt the Butter:**
   - In a large skillet over medium heat, melt the butter.
2. **Add the Garlic:**
   - Add the minced garlic and cook for 1-2 minutes, until fragrant.
3. **Add the Cream:**
   - Pour in the heavy cream and bring to a simmer. Cook for 5 minutes, stirring constantly.
4. **Add the Cheese:**
   - Gradually add the grated Parmesan cheese, whisking until the sauce is smooth and

creamy. Season with salt, black pepper, and nutmeg (if using).

5. **Serve:**
    o Serve the Alfredo sauce over fettuccine or your favorite pasta. Garnish with fresh parsley if desired.

Nutritional Information (per serving):

- Calories: 450
- Carbohydrates: 5g
- Protein: 12g
- Fat: 44g
- Fiber: 0g
- Sugar: 1g
- Sodium: 700mg

Tips:

- Use freshly grated Parmesan cheese for the best flavor and texture.
- For a lighter version, substitute half-and-half for the heavy cream.
- Store leftovers in an airtight container in the refrigerator for up to 3 days.

Pesto Sauce

Prep Time: 10 minutes
Cook Time: 0 minutes
Servings: 4 servings

Ingredients:

- 2 cups fresh basil leaves
- 1/2 cup grated Parmesan cheese
- 1/2 cup extra virgin olive oil
- 1/4 cup pine nuts
- 2 cloves garlic, minced
- 1/2 tsp salt
- 1/4 tsp black pepper

Instructions:

1. **Blend the Ingredients:**
   - In a food processor, combine the basil leaves, Parmesan cheese, pine nuts, and garlic. Pulse until finely chopped.
2. **Add the Olive Oil:**
   - With the food processor running, slowly pour in the olive oil until the mixture is smooth. Season with salt and black pepper to taste.
3. **Adjust Consistency:**
   - If the pesto is too thick, add a little more olive oil or a splash of water to reach the desired consistency.
4. Serve the pesto sauce over pasta, as a spread on sandwiches, or as a dip for vegetables.

Nutritional Information (per serving):

- Calories: 300
- Carbohydrates: 3g
- Protein: 6g
- Fat: 30g
- Fiber: 1g
- Sugar: 0g
- Sodium: 400mg

Tips:

- For a nuttier flavor, toast the pine nuts before blending.
- Substitute walnuts or almonds for pine nuts for a different twist.
- Store pesto in an airtight container in the refrigerator for up to 1 week or freeze for up to 3 months.

BBQ Sauce

Prep Time: 10 minutes
Cook Time: 20 minutes
Servings: 4 servings
Ingredients:
- 1 cup ketchup
- 1/2 cup apple cider vinegar
- 1/2 cup brown sugar, packed
- 1/4 cup honey
- 1 tbsp Worcestershire sauce
- 1 tbsp lemon juice
- 1 tbsp Dijon mustard
- 1 tsp smoked paprika
- 1 tsp garlic powder
- 1/2 tsp onion powder
- 1/2 tsp black pepper
- 1/4 tsp cayenne pepper (optional)

Instructions:
1. **Combine the Ingredients:**
   - In a medium saucepan, combine the ketchup, apple cider vinegar, brown sugar, honey, Worcestershire sauce, lemon juice, and Dijon mustard.
2. **Add the Spices:**
   - Stir in the smoked paprika, garlic powder, onion powder, black pepper, and cayenne pepper (if using).
3. **Simmer the Sauce:**

- o Bring the mixture to a simmer over medium heat. Reduce the heat to low and let it simmer for 20 minutes, stirring occasionally.
4. **Adjust Seasoning:**
   - o Taste and adjust seasoning as needed. Add more vinegar for tanginess or more sugar for sweetness.
5. **Serve:**
   - o Use the BBQ sauce immediately, or let it cool and store in an airtight container in the refrigerator for up to 2 weeks.

Nutritional Information (per serving):
- Calories: 200
- Carbohydrates: 53g
- Protein: 1g
- Fat: 0g
- Fiber: 0g
- Sugar: 49g
- Sodium: 700mg

Tips:
- For a smoky flavor, add a few drops of liquid smoke.
- Use the sauce as a marinade, baste, or dipping sauce for grilled meats and vegetables.
- Customize the heat level by adjusting the amount of cayenne pepper.

Cheese Sauce

Prep Time: 5 minutes
Cook Time: 10 minutes
Servings: 4 servings

Ingredients:

- 2 tbsp unsalted butter
- 2 tbsp all-purpose flour
- 1 1/2 cups whole milk
- 1 1/2 cups shredded cheddar cheese
- 1/2 tsp salt
- 1/4 tsp black pepper
- 1/4 tsp ground mustard (optional)
- 1/8 tsp cayenne pepper (optional)

Instructions:

1. **Make the Roux:**
   - In a medium saucepan over medium heat, melt the butter. Add the flour and whisk constantly for about 2 minutes, until the mixture is bubbly and lightly golden.

2. **Add the Milk:**
   - Gradually whisk in the milk. Continue whisking until the mixture is smooth and begins to thicken, about 3-5 minutes.

3. **Add the Cheese:**
   - Reduce the heat to low. Stir in the shredded cheddar cheese, salt, black pepper, ground mustard (if using), and cayenne pepper (if

using). Stir until the cheese is completely melted and the sauce is smooth.

4. **Serve:**

   o Serve the cheese sauce immediately over vegetables, pasta, or as a dip for pretzels and chips.

Nutritional Information (per serving):

- Calories: 250
- Carbohydrates: 7g
- Protein: 12g
- Fat: 20g
- Fiber: 0g
- Sugar: 4g
- Sodium: 400mg

Tips:

- Use sharp cheddar cheese for a more intense flavor.
- For a smoother sauce, grate the cheese yourself rather than using pre-shredded cheese.
- Add a pinch of smoked paprika for a smoky flavor.

Tzatziki

Prep Time: 15 minutes
Cook Time: 0 minutes
Servings: 4 servings
Ingredients:

- 1 cup Greek yogurt
- 1 cucumber, peeled, seeded, and grated
- 2 cloves garlic, minced
- 1 tbsp olive oil
- 1 tbsp fresh lemon juice
- 1 tbsp chopped fresh dill
- 1/2 tsp salt
- 1/4 tsp black pepper

Instructions:

1. **Prepare the Cucumber:**
   o Place the grated cucumber in a clean kitchen towel and squeeze out as much excess moisture as possible.
2. **Mix the Ingredients:**
   o In a medium bowl, combine the Greek yogurt, grated cucumber, minced garlic, olive oil, lemon juice, chopped dill, salt, and black pepper.
3. **Stir Until Combined:**
   o Mix well until all ingredients are thoroughly combined.

4. **Adjust Seasoning:**
   - Taste and adjust seasoning as needed. Add more salt, lemon juice, or dill to taste.
5. **Serve:**
   - Serve the tzatziki immediately, or cover and refrigerate for at least 1 hour to let the flavors meld.

Nutritional Information (per serving):
- Calories: 80
- Carbohydrates: 4g
- Protein: 4g
- Fat: 6g
- Fiber: 0g
- Sugar: 3g
- Sodium: 300mg

Tips:
- For a thicker tzatziki, use strained Greek yogurt or strain regular yogurt through a cheesecloth.
- Serve as a dip with pita bread, as a sauce for gyros, or as a side with grilled meats and vegetables.
- Store in an airtight container in the refrigerator for up to 3 days.

FROSTINGS AND FILLINGS

Buttercream Frosting

Prep Time: 10 minutes
Cook Time: 0 minutes
Servings: Frosts 12 cupcakes or a 9-inch cake
Ingredients:
- 1 cup unsalted butter, softened
- 4 cups powdered sugar, sifted
- 1/4 cup heavy cream or milk
- 2 tsp vanilla extract
- Pinch of salt

Instructions:
1. **Beat the Butter:**
   o In the bowl of your KitchenAid stand mixer, beat the softened butter on medium speed until creamy and smooth, about 2 minutes.
2. **Add the Powdered Sugar:**
   o Gradually add the powdered sugar, 1 cup at a time, beating on low speed after each addition until well incorporated.
3. **Add the Liquid Ingredients:**
   o Add the heavy cream or milk, vanilla extract, and a pinch of salt. Increase the speed to medium-high and beat for an additional 3 minutes, until the frosting is light and fluffy.

4. **Adjust Consistency:**
   - If the frosting is too thick, add more cream or milk, 1 tablespoon at a time, until the desired consistency is reached. If the frosting is too thin, add more powdered sugar, 1/4 cup at a time.
5. **Use Immediately:**
   - Frost cupcakes or cake as desired. If not using immediately, store in an airtight container in the refrigerator for up to 1 week. Re-whip before using.

Nutritional Information (per serving):
- Calories: 250
- Carbohydrates: 32g
- Protein: 0g
- Fat: 14g
- Fiber: 0g
- Sugar: 32g
- Sodium: 20mg

Tips:
- For flavored buttercream, add a few drops of your favorite extract, such as almond, lemon, or peppermint.
- To create colored frosting, add a few drops of food coloring and mix until combined.
- For a chocolate version, add 1/2 cup of unsweetened cocoa powder along with the powdered sugar.

Cream Cheese Frosting

Prep Time: 10 minutes
Cook Time: 0 minutes
Servings: Frosts 12 cupcakes or a 9-inch cake

Ingredients:

- 1/2 cup unsalted butter, softened
- 8 oz cream cheese, softened
- 4 cups powdered sugar, sifted
- 2 tsp vanilla extract
- Pinch of salt

Instructions:

1. **Beat the Butter and Cream Cheese:**
   - In the bowl of your KitchenAid stand mixer, beat the softened butter and cream cheese on medium speed until smooth and creamy, about 2 minutes.

2. **Add the Powdered Sugar:**
   - Gradually add the powdered sugar, 1 cup at a time, beating on low speed after each addition until well incorporated.

3. **Add the Vanilla and Salt:**
   - Add the vanilla extract and a pinch of salt. Increase the speed to medium-high and beat for an additional 2-3 minutes, until the frosting is light and fluffy.

4. **Adjust Consistency:**
   - If the frosting is too thick, add a tablespoon of milk or cream. If the frosting is too thin,

add more powdered sugar, 1/4 cup at a time, until the desired consistency is reached.

5. **Use Immediately:**
   - ○ Frost cupcakes or cake as desired. If not using immediately, store in an airtight container in the refrigerator for up to 1 week. Re-whip before using.

Nutritional Information (per serving):

- Calories: 270
- Carbohydrates: 32g
- Protein: 1g
- Fat: 16g
- Fiber: 0g
- Sugar: 31g
- Sodium: 90mg

Tips:

- For a tangier frosting, add a teaspoon of lemon juice.
- To make a chocolate cream cheese frosting, add 1/2 cup of unsweetened cocoa powder along with the powdered sugar.
- Ensure both the butter and cream cheese are fully softened to avoid lumps in the frosting.

Chocolate Ganache

Prep Time: 5 minutes
Cook Time: 10 minutes
Servings: Makes about 2 cups

Ingredients:
- 8 oz semi-sweet or dark chocolate, finely chopped
- 1 cup heavy cream
- 1 tbsp unsalted butter (optional, for shine)

Instructions:
1. **Heat the Cream:**
   - In a small saucepan, heat the heavy cream over medium heat until it begins to simmer. Do not let it boil.
2. **Combine with Chocolate:**
   - Place the chopped chocolate in a heatproof bowl. Pour the hot cream over the chocolate and let it sit for 2-3 minutes to melt the chocolate.
3. **Stir Until Smooth:**
   - Gently stir the mixture with a whisk or spatula until the chocolate is completely melted and the ganache is smooth. If using, stir in the butter until melted and combined.
4. **Cool to Desired Consistency:**
   - For a pourable ganache, let it cool slightly before using. For a spreadable consistency, let it cool to room temperature or refrigerate, stirring occasionally, until it thickens.

5. **Use as Desired:**
   - ○ Use the ganache to glaze cakes, cupcakes, or as a filling for pastries. Store any leftover ganache in an airtight container in the refrigerator for up to 1 week. Reheat gently before using.

Nutritional Information (per serving):
- Calories: 140
- Carbohydrates: 12g
- Protein: 1g
- Fat: 10g
- Fiber: 2g
- Sugar: 9g
- Sodium: 10mg

Tips:
- Use high-quality chocolate for the best flavor and texture.
- For a flavored ganache, add a tablespoon of your favorite liqueur or extract (such as vanilla or almond) along with the cream.
- If the ganache separates or appears grainy, whisk in a teaspoon of warm water until it becomes smooth again.

Lemon Curd

Prep Time: 10 minutes
Cook Time: 15 minutes
Servings: Makes about 2 cups
Ingredients:

- 1 cup granulated sugar
- 3 large eggs
- 1/2 cup fresh lemon juice (about 2-3 lemons)
- 1 tbsp lemon zest
- 1/2 cup unsalted butter, cubed

Instructions:

1. **Prepare a Double Boiler:**
   - Fill a medium saucepan with about 2 inches of water and bring to a simmer. Place a heatproof bowl over the saucepan, ensuring the bottom of the bowl does not touch the water.

2. **Whisk the Ingredients:**
   - In the heatproof bowl, whisk together the sugar and eggs until smooth. Add the lemon juice and zest, and whisk to combine.

3. **Cook the Mixture:**
   - Place the bowl over the simmering water. Cook the mixture, whisking constantly, until it thickens and coats the back of a spoon, about 10-15 minutes. The temperature should reach about 170°F (77°C).

4. **Add the Butter:**

- o Remove the bowl from the heat and stir in the butter, one piece at a time, until fully melted and combined.

5. **Strain and Cool:**
   - o Strain the lemon curd through a fine-mesh sieve into a clean bowl to remove any lumps or zest. Cover the surface with plastic wrap, pressing it directly onto the curd to prevent a skin from forming.

6. **Refrigerate:**
   - o Refrigerate the lemon curd until completely chilled, at least 2 hours. The curd will continue to thicken as it cools.

Nutritional Information (per serving):
- Calories: 100
- Carbohydrates: 10g
- Protein: 1g
- Fat: 6g
- Fiber: 0g
- Sugar: 10g
- Sodium: 10mg

Tips:
- Use freshly squeezed lemon juice for the best flavor.
- Lemon curd can be stored in an airtight container in the refrigerator for up to 1 week.
- Use lemon curd as a filling for cakes, tarts, or pastries, or spread it on scones or toast.

Pastry Cream

Prep Time: 10 minutes
Cook Time: 10 minutes
Servings: Makes about 2 cups
Ingredients:
- 2 cups whole milk
- 1/2 cup granulated sugar
- 1/4 cup cornstarch
- 4 large egg yolks
- 2 tsp vanilla extract
- 2 tbsp unsalted butter

Instructions:
1. **Heat the Milk:**
   - In a medium saucepan, heat the milk over medium heat until it begins to simmer. Do not let it boil.
2. **Whisk the Dry Ingredients:**
   - In a medium bowl, whisk together the sugar and cornstarch until well combined.
3. **Add the Egg Yolks:**
   - Add the egg yolks to the sugar mixture and whisk until smooth and pale in color.
4. **Temper the Egg Mixture:**
   - Gradually pour about 1/2 cup of the hot milk into the egg mixture, whisking constantly to temper the eggs. Slowly pour the tempered egg mixture back into the saucepan with the remaining milk, whisking constantly.
5. **Cook the Pastry Cream:**

- Cook the mixture over medium heat, whisking constantly, until it thickens and comes to a boil, about 2-3 minutes. Continue to cook for an additional 1-2 minutes to ensure the cornstarch is fully cooked.

6. **Add the Butter and Vanilla:** Remove the saucepan from the heat and stir in the butter and vanilla extract until smooth.

7. **Strain and Cool:** Strain the pastry cream through a fine-mesh sieve into a clean bowl to remove any lumps. Cover the surface with plastic wrap, pressing it directly onto the cream to prevent a skin from forming.

8. Refrigerate the pastry cream until completely chilled, at least 2 hours. The cream will thicken as it cools.

Nutritional Information (per serving):

- Calories: 150
- Carbohydrates: 21g
- Protein: 3g
- Fat: 6g
- Fiber: 0g
- Sugar: 17g
- Sodium: 30mg

Tips:

- For a richer flavor, use a combination of milk and heavy cream.
- Pastry cream can be stored in an airtight container in the refrigerator for up to 3 days.
- Use pastry cream as a filling for éclairs, cream puffs, tarts, or as a layer in cakes and trifles.

CONCLUSION

Thank you for joining me on this culinary journey with the KitchenAid Stand Mixer. As we've explored the endless possibilities this incredible tool offers, I hope you've discovered the joy and simplicity of creating delicious homemade recipes. Each recipe in this cookbook is designed to bring a little more love and warmth into your kitchen.

From the warmth of freshly baked bread to the sweetness of perfect cookies, the elegance of beautifully frosted cakes, and the delight of homemade ice cream, you've learned how to transform simple ingredients into extraordinary dishes. Each creation is a testament to the magic that happens when you combine passion with the right tools.

Your KitchenAid Stand Mixer is more than just a kitchen appliance; it's a gateway to creativity and flavor. Whether you're kneading dough for a hearty loaf of bread, mixing batter for a celebratory cake, or churning out fresh pasta for a family dinner, this mixer is your reliable companion, making the process easier and more enjoyable. Its versatility allows you to try a wide range of recipes, from dips and sauces to doughs and frostings, ensuring that every meal can be a special occasion.

I hope this cookbook has inspired you to experiment, to try new things, and to feel confident in your abilities. Cooking is not just about feeding the body but also nourishing the soul, creating memories, and sharing love through food. Each recipe is a starting point for your culinary adventures.

Don't be afraid to tweak and adjust them to your taste. Add your favorite spices, substitute ingredients, and make each dish your own.

Remember to take care of your KitchenAid Stand Mixer. Regular cleaning and proper maintenance will ensure it serves you well for years to come. Refer to the user manual for tips on keeping it in top condition, and don't hesitate to explore additional attachments that can further expand its capabilities.

As you continue to explore and create, remember that the best meals are made with heart. So, keep mixing, kneading, and blending, and may your kitchen be filled with laughter, delicious aromas, and the joy of sharing good food with loved ones.

Cooking together can be a wonderful way to bond, and the satisfaction of making something from scratch is truly unmatched.

Thank you for choosing this cookbook. I am excited for all the wonderful dishes you will create and the memories you will make. Happy cooking.

Made in the USA
Columbia, SC
21 October 2024

44815294R00120